equal op[illegible]
in farm programs

AN APPRAISAL OF SERVICES RENDERED BY AGENCIES OF THE UNITED STATES DEPARTMENT OF AGRICULTURE

A Report of the United States Commission on Civil Rights

1965

For sale by the Superintendent of Documents, U.S. Government Printing Office
Washington, D.C., 20402 - Price 60 cents

LETTER OF TRANSMITTAL

THE UNITED STATES COMMISSION ON CIVIL RIGHTS,
Washington, D.C., February 27, 1965.

THE PRESIDENT
THE PRESIDENT OF THE SENATE
THE SPEAKER OF THE HOUSE OF REPRESENTATIVES

SIRS:

The Commission on Civil Rights presents to you this report pursuant to Public Law 85–315, as amended.

This report is a study of selected programs of the U.S. Department of Agriculture designed to alleviate problems among the rural population, and, in particular, among the rural population of the South. The Commission has found serious matters of concern and need for corrective action, but it is heartening to note the increasing awareness among Department officials of the need for change.

We urge your consideration of the facts presented and of the recommendations for corrective action.

Respectfully yours,

JOHN A. HANNAH, *Chairman*
EUGENE PATTERSON, *Vice Chairman*
MRS. FRANKIE M. FREEMAN
ERWIN N. GRISWOLD
REV. THEODORE M. HESBURGH, C.S.C.
ROBERT S. RANKIN

ACKNOWLEDGMENTS

This report would not have been possible without the cooperation of many private citizens and government officials, Federal, State, and local. Secretary of Agriculture Orville L. Freeman made available the resources of his Department and the Commission has uniformly received cooperation and assistance from every agency of the Department. The evaluation and interpretation of the Commission's findings were greatly strengthened through the generous assistance provided by the administrators of departmental programs and their staffs.

Particular mention should be made of officials in those States and counties of the South where racial feelings were running high during the period of our study. These officials received Commission field staff with courtesy, provided helpful information, and frequently readjusted busy schedules to facilitate the work of the Commission.

The Commission is indebted to its staff which has continued to move forward with thoughtful purpose and constructive effort. During the past year, the Acting Staff Director, Howard W. Rogerson, has provided stability and leadership to the staff and able and dedicated service to the Commission itself.

CONTENTS

II. THE COOPERATION EXTENSION SERVICE—Con.

PREFACE

The U.S. Commission on Civil Rights is a temporary, independent, bipartisan agency established by Congress in 1957 and directed to

- Investigate complaints alleging that citizens are being deprived of their right to vote by reason of their race, color, religion, or national origin, or by reason of fraudulent practices;
- Study and collect information concerning legal developments constituting a denial of equal protection of the laws under the Constitution;
- Appraise Federal laws and policies with respect to equal protection of the laws;
- Serve as a national clearinghouse for information in respect to denials of equal protection of the laws; and
- Submit reports, findings, and recommendations to the President and the Congress.

Pursuant to its statutory mandate, the Commission has conducted studies of programs administered by many agencies of the Federal Government. These studies have considered activities of the Departments of Labor, Defense, Interior, Commerce, and Health, Education, and Welfare; and of the Housing and Home Finance Agency, Atomic Energy Commission, National Science Foundation, Federal Aviation Agency, and the President's Committees on Government Employment and on Government Contracts. Reports containing detailed findings and recommendations in the various areas of Commission study have been submitted to the Congress and the President.[1]

[1] *A Catalog of Publications* of the U.S. Commission on Civil Rights and of its State Advisory Committees is available from the Commission. All printed Commission publications are available at Government Printing Office depository libraries throughout the country or from the U.S. Commission on Civil Rights Library on interlibrary loan.

The Commission has not previously appraised the programs administered by the Department of Agriculture, though the 1960 report *Equal Protection of the Laws in Public Higher Education* touched briefly on the subject. The Commission decided to review the programs and policies of the Department with respect to denials of equal protection of the laws because of the importance of these programs and policies to the rural population of our nation and their direct relevance to the problems of rural poverty.

From the outset the objective of the study was to determine whether there are discriminatory policies, practices, or patterns inherent in the administration of selected programs which result in the denial of Federal benefits to persons because of their race or color. It is not the purpose of this study to pursue individual complaints of discrimination or to document particular instances of equality of opportunity; nor is it the function of the Commission to evaluate basic agricultural policies of the Federal Government.

Instances of discrimination revealed by Commission staff investigations were brought to the attention of the Department of Agriculture and the Department has taken measures to correct some of the abuses and inequities reported. Following the passage of the Civil Rights Act of 1964, Secretary Freeman convened a meeting of State directors and top administrative personnel of Department agencies. At this meeting he stated that he expected agencies to comply with the letter and the spirit of the Civil Rights Act and to develop immediate programs of affirmative action for its implementation. Individual administrators of agencies within the Department subsequently met with State officials to explain to them the requirements of the Act.

Certain regulations implementing the Act have now been issued and other policy changes are being formulated. It is yet too early to assess fully the effect of these recently adopted policies.

METHODS OF STUDY AND DEFINITIONS

This study focused on the extent and quality of services rendered to Negro rural families by the agencies of the Department of Agriculture which provide direct service at the county level. These included the Farmers Home Administration (FHA), the Soil Conservation Service (SCS), the Agricultural Stabilization and Conservation Service (ASCS), and the Federal Extension Service (FES). A considerably more detailed study was made of the Extension Service because of its key role as the educational arm of the Department and because of its position in the line of communication between other agencies of the Federal Government and farmers. Furthermore, its programs for youth and homemakers provided more diverse services than those of any other agency of the Department.

The study was concerned particularly with an evaluation of the services rendered Negroes in counties where Negroes formed a significant portion of the varying potential clientele of the agencies and where such services, therefore, logically could be expected.

Research techniques used in the study included conferences and interviews with program administrators and experts from private and State universities in the fields of agricultural economics, extension education, statistics, demography, and public administration; staff field trips; review and evaluation of program material; and statistical analyses of service data.

Interviews and conferences were held with some 50 officials and staff of the Department of Agriculture and other Federal agencies in Washington. These discussions provided a basic understanding of the overall policies of the Department and of the purposes and methods of operation of the agencies under review. The meetings were helpful in the collection and interpretation of data.

Field trips made by the Commission staff provided valuable information on the administration of programs being studied. Between March and August 1964, Commission staff visited State offices of one or more of the agencies in 6 States and county offices in 22 counties in 8 Southern States.[1] During these trips 177 agricultural officials, committeemen, farmers, and others were interviewed.[2] These field visits and interviews were designed to reach counties with varied crops and economies served by different agencies and personnel of the Department of Agriculture. The conditions described in the following report are, unless otherwise noted, based upon information secured during field visits and interviews, transcripts of which are contained in Commission files.

Material on service submitted by the several agencies, including departmental reports, State and county reports, plans, and statistics, was examined and evaluated to determine whether the various programs were being administered equally for whites and Negroes. Because 98 percent of all Negro farm operators in the United States are located in Southern States,[3] the study concentrated on how programs of the selected agencies operate in the South. With the cooperation of the Economic Research Service of the Department of Agriculture, those counties were identified in which nonwhites were either the majority of farm owners or the owner-operators of 15 percent or more of total farm land in 1959. In most States the three counties with the greatest number of nonwhite owner-

---

[1] Alabama, Arkansas, Georgia, Mississippi, Louisiana, North Carolina, South Carolina, and Virginia.

[2] During the course of field visits, interviews were held with 12 Soil Conservation Service staff at the county and State levels; 23 interviews with county and State Farmers Home Administration personnel and 7 FHA county committeemen; 9 county and State staff of the Agricultural Stabilization and Conservation Service and 3 with ASCS county committeemen; 52 county and home demonstration agents of the Cooperative Extension Service, representing 23 counties, and interviews with 34 State staff of extension services for 6 States, including 5 State extension directors. Six interviews were held with officials of other State and Federal agencies and some 30 private individuals, including farmers, ministers, businessmen, professors, and representatives of private organizations.

[3] *1957 Agriculture Census,* vol. II, ch. X, table 31, p. 1163.

operated farms were added if not otherwise included. This produced a list of 71 counties in 14 Southern States. Data on programs in some of these counties were submitted to statistical analysis, using appropriate census figures for determination of numbers of persons in the class to which service was rendered. Since the Cooperative Extension Service is an educational agency geared to the rural population as a whole, and not just the farmers, rural households and rural youth were considered one proper measure of potential clientele, while for agricultural service only number of farm operators were counted. The Soil Conservation Service, on the other hand, works primarily with owners of land and thus the number of owner-operators of farms was considered an appropriate measure of potential clientele. The Farmers Home Administration aids both owners and tenants, and the Agricultural Stabilization and Conservation Service administers crop allotments which reach every tenure group, so that all farm operators were an appropriate measure for these services.

The precise method of analysis is explained in the text with the presentation of conclusions. Generally, however, it should be noted that the most recent census figures—the *1959 Agriculture Census* and the *1960 Census of Population*—have been used extensively in the study. Where program data for 1963 or 1964 were compared with census figures for 1959 or 1960, the comparisons do not reflect the changes which have taken place in the five years since the census enumeration.

Definition of Terms

Farmer—Farmer as used here refers to the several tenure groups defined by the Bureau of the Census as "Farm Operators" and includes 1) "full owners;" 2) "part owners," who operate land they own and rent additional farm land; 3) "managers," who operate land for others and are paid a wage or salary for their services; and 4) "tenants," who rent all the land they operate for cash or shares of the crop.

Tenants—Tenants are classified by the census on the basis of rental arrangements in regard to the payment of cash rent, sharing of crops, sharing of livestock or livestock products, and the furnishing of equipment by the landlord. They include cash tenants, share-cash tenants, crop-share tenants, and livestock-share tenants, and croppers.

Croppers—Croppers differ from other tenants in that they are dependent on the landlord to furnish all of the work animals or tractor power and work under the close supervision of the landowners or their agents.

South—When reference is to census figures for the South, the 16 States included in that geographical area are Alabama, Arkansas, Delaware, Florida, Georgia, Kentucky, Louisiana, Maryland, Mississippi, North Carolina, Oklahoma, South Carolina, Tennessee, Texas, West Virginia, Virginia, and the District of Columbia. When fewer States are discussed, they are identified in the footnotes.

Nonwhite—The Bureau of the Census has established two "color" classifications—"white" and "nonwhite." Nonwhite includes Negroes, American Indians, Japanese, Chinese, Filipinos, Koreans, Hawaiians, Asian Indians, Malayans, Eskimos, Aleuts, etc. Since Negroes constitute 92 percent of all the nonwhites, the use of "nonwhite" and Negro in this report can be considered synonymous except for several counties in North Carolina and in Oklahoma where there are Indians. Persons of Mexican birth or ancestry who are not definitely of Indian or other nonwhite race are classified as white by the census.

I. THE PROBLEM IN PERSPECTIVE

The position of the Negro farmer in America has been dictated to a large extent by the economic and social history of the South and particularly by the problems of Southern agriculture.[1] The nature of these problems can be seen in the fact that the need for agricultural reform has been a recurrent regional theme and that for decades proposals to bring into being "the New South" have included land ownership, crop diversification, and soil conservation.[2] Many of the South's agricultural troubles have long been seen as the lingering legacy of a plantation system based on the dominance of cotton in its social and economic life.

While rural America has shared less than our cities in the benefits of national economic advances, Southern agriculture has been even less fortunate and in the rural South the Negroes have benefitted least. Among the problems inherent in the plantation economy were a tenancy system founded on exploitation of the Negro and a credit system which made it almost impossible for small farmers to obtain loans for expansion or for tenants to purchase land. The cultivation of cotton year after year without rotation of crops had severe consequences for the soil. The Southern farmer found it increasingly difficult to earn a living from eroded and depleted land. Beginning in the 1890's the ravages of the boll weevil became a major problem for cotton growers, striking with most

---

[1] See Blair, Lewis H. (C. Vann Woodward, ed.), *A Southern Prophecy: The Prosperity of the South Dependent Upon the Elevation of the Negro* (1899) (Boston: Little, Brown, 1964).

[2] See Myrdal, Gunnar, *An American Dilemma* (New York; Harper & Bros., 1944), pp. 230–231, *et passim.*

disastrous effect in those areas where the majority of farmers were Negroes.[3] These factors, together with the growing demand for industrial labor in the expanding factories of the North, prompted an exodus from Southern agriculture which has never been reversed.[4]

THE SEARCH FOR SOLUTIONS

For over a hundred years the United States Department of Agriculture (USDA) has administered programs designed to meet chronic problems in agriculture and to improve the life of rural America.[5] No segment of the rural population experienced those problems more acutely or stood in greater need of the Department's assistance than the Negro farmer and his family.

The Great Depression of the 1930's and the drastic drop in world cotton prices created hardships more severe for Southern agriculture than for the country as a whole and brought increased concern on the part of the Federal Government. The New Deal search for solutions to agricultural problems brought about basic reforms in the credit system. Programs restricting the amount of land in production of cotton and other crops, coupled with price supports, were designed to achieve a better balance between supply and demand. Legislation aimed at improving the position of the

[3] *Id.*, pp. 227–229, 231–235.

[4] Number of farm operators in South by color and tenure (in thousands):

	White			*Nonwhite*		
	1935	*1959*	*Percent change*	*1935*	*1959*	*Percent change*
All farm operators	2, 606	1, 379	−47	815	266	−67
Full owners	1, 190	857	−28	150	90	−40
Part owners	200	285	+43	36	37	+2.8
Tenants	1, 202	228	−81	629	138	−78

Source: *1959 Agriculture Census*, vol. II, ch. X, table 5. See also Population Reference Bureau, Inc., *Population Bulletin*, XIX, No. 3 (May 1963), p. 53.

[5] For a detailed discussion of the development of programs and agencies of the Department of Agriculture, see *Century of Service: The First 100 Years of the U.S. Department of Agriculture*, Economic Research Service, USDA (Washington: U.S. Government Printing Office, 1963).

tenant farmer was enacted, emergency soil conservation practices were put into effect, and programs to encourage crop diversification and land ownership were launched.

While some programs were to be administered by the Federal Government through the Department of Agriculture and some by the States with Federal financial assistance, most were based on the principle of local consent and were dependent on local committees for the shaping of important policy decisions.

Of the programs developed in the 20th century the Extension Service was among the first to receive Congressional authorization for Federal-State cooperation. State extension programs receiving Federal assistance were designed to educate farm and rural families in better farming practices and improved health and nutrition.[6] Other current programs reaching the individual farmer on the county level were originally designed in the 1930's. The Farmers Home Administration helps farmers acquire land, equipment and operating funds, and seeks to improve farm and money management through its programs of low-cost credit and technical assistance.[7] To attack the problems of soil exhaustion and erosion, the Soil Conservation Service has organized conservation districts throughout the nation and has set out to save the precious soil.[8] Production restraints reinforced by price supports are administered by the Agricultural Stabilization and Conservation Service.[9] Rural electrification, farmers cooperatives, forestry, agricultural research and experimentation, and marketing research and assistance all are the subject of Federal programs within the Department of Agriculture.[10]

---

[6] Department of Agriculture, *A Guide to Extension Programs for the Future: The Scope and Responsibilities of the Cooperative Extension Service* (Extension Committee on Organization and Policy), July 1959. Hereinafter cited as the *Scope Report 1959*.

[7] U.S. Department of Agriculture, *Loan Programs of the Farmers Home Administration* (June 1962), pp. 1–3; *Farmers Home Administration in Brief* (USDA Publication PA 547, January 1963, revised February 1964).

[8] U.S. Department of Agriculture, *What the Soil Conservation Service Does* (SCS–C1–3, revised September 1963).

[9] U.S. Department of Agriculture, *A Guide to Understanding the U.S. Department of Agriculture* (USDA Office of Personnel, revised October 1963).

[10] *Ibid.*

Through these and other programs the Department of Agriculture has sought to break the cycle of rural poverty. Every aspect of the farmer's life has been touched. Religion has been called into play by the institution of soil stewardship and by the close association of Extension education with church work. The youth have been organized into 4-H clubs to learn good farming practices early. Farm mothers have been trained in better family living, housekeeping, health, and family care.[11] Millions of dollars—and thousands of Federal, State, and local employees—are committed to the struggle to improve farm life and productivity.

As a result of these efforts the Department of Agriculture, in cooperation with the land-grant colleges and State and local governments, has been instrumental in raising the economic, educational, and social levels of thousands of farm and rural families. The agencies of the Department can be proud of much that they have accomplished over the past 30 years. Nevertheless, the advances made by farm and rural families have not been enjoyed by all and especially not by Negro rural families concentrated in the South.[12]

Aided by Federal loans and technical advice, a large percentage of the South's white farmers have increasingly diversified their crops and applied modern farming practices, so that in 1959 slightly less than half were dependent upon the traditional row crops—cotton, tobacco, and peanuts.[13] Concomitant gains have been made in arresting soil exhaustion and erosion. Southern white farmers have raised their incomes, increased the size of their farms, improved their housing, and advanced their education.[14]

A quarter of a million Negro farmers stand as a glaring exception to this picture of progress. While diversification in crops and

---

[11] *Century of Service, op. cit.*, pp. 82, 400; Alfred Charles True, *A History of Agricultural Extension Work in the United States, 1785–1923*, USDA Misc. Publ. No. 15 (Washington: U.S. Government Printing Office, 1928), pp. 129–131; U.S. Department of Agriculture, "People's Souls and Soil," *Soil Conservation*, May 1964, p. 237.

[12] According to the 1960 Census, 93 percent of rural Negroes resided in the South. *1960 Census of Population*, PC(2)–1C, Nonwhite Population by Race, table I, p. 1.

[13] *1959 Agriculture Census*, vol. I, State table 19. Computation based on number of farms counted as cotton farms, tobacco farms, other field crop farms, and general farms.

[14] See notes 23, 30, 33, and 37 *infra*.

livestock has generally given the Southern white farmer a broader and more stable economic base,[15] 92 percent of Negro commercial farms still derive more than 50 percent of their income from cotton, tobacco, and peanuts.[16]

Mechanization, far from promoting the Negro farmer's welfare, has been a major factor in his displacement.[17] Limited gains in farm income, size of farm, living conditions, and educational level during the last ten years have not lessened significantly the disadvantaged status of the Negro farmer. Most Negroes on farms continue to live at a minimum subsistence level.[18] The social and economic gap between white and Negro rural and farm populations continues to widen. Although many poor white families are found in the Southern States, the concentration of characteristics of deprivation among Negro families is especially intense. Among rural Negro families 62 percent had less than $2,000 income in 1959 compared to only 26 percent of white rural families. The disadvantaged position of Negro families is greatly increased by the fact that the average rural Negro family was one-third larger than rural white families.[19]

THE FARM FAMILY

One and a half million Negroes lived in Southern farm families in 1960 as did 4.4 million whites.[20] The economic distance sepa-

[15] *1959 Agriculture Census,* vols. I and II.

[16] *Id.,* vol. I, State table 19. See note 13, *supra.*

[17] Population Reference Bureau, *op. cit.,* pp. 63, 73.

[18] Dr. Oscar Ornati, *Poverty in America,* A Report for the National Policy Committee on Pockets of Poverty (Washington: National Policy Committee on Pockets of Poverty, March 1964), p. 3.

[19] *1960 Census of Population,* PC(1)–1C, U.S. Summary, tables 248 and 266.

[20] *1960 Census of Population,* PC(2)–1C, Nonwhite Population by Race, table I, p. 1; *1960 Census of Population,* PC(1)–1C, U.S. Summary, table 107; p. 250. The Bureau of the Census and the Economic Research Service of the Department of Agriculture agree that this 1960 population census figure is probably too low. They agree that the estimate of the *Current Population Survey* of about 2,450,000 nonwhite farm population in the South for the same date is a more accurate figure. *Letter from USDA, ERS to Commission on Civil Rights,* December 4, 1964. Because the *Current Population Survey* contains no State data or characteristics by color other than age and sex, the Commission found it necessary to use the 1960 population census data in making analyses of social and economic conditions of farm people.

761-685 O—65——2

rating Negro and white farm families is clearly illustrated by the fact that in 1959 the highest average level of living index for Negro farmers in any of the 14 States studied was lower than the lowest State average level of living index of white farmers.[21]

While Negroes have traditionally operated smaller farms than whites, the discrepancy in size was larger in 1960 than in 1950.

Average acreage per farm by race for the South [22]

	1950	*1959*
White	175.3	249.0
Nonwhite	47.0	52.3
Difference	128.3	196.7

Even white cropper-operated farms (economically the lowest tenure class) averaged 68 acres while farms operated by Negro full owners had an average of only 62 acres.[23] Although Negroes in 1959 comprised 16 percent of the farm operators of the South, they operated less than 4 percent of the farm land.[24]

Only a handful of Southern Negro farmers operate economically viable farms [25]—1.3 percent compared to 13.7 percent of the white

[21] Measures used in this index were: (1) average dollar value per farm of land and buildings; (2) average dollar value per farm of sale of products; and (3) possession of three common household items—telephone, home freezer, and car. The highest State level-of-living index for nonwhite farm operators among the Southern States (Maryland) was less than the lowest State index for white operators (Kentucky). The 1959 nonwhite indexes ranged from 30 in Mississippi to 67 in Maryland, while the white indexes ranged from 71 in Kentucky to 116 in Maryland. The 1959 national average of all counties was 100. J. D. Cowhig and C. L. Beale, "Socio-economic Differences Between White and Nonwhite Farm Populations of the South," *Social Forces,* vol. 42, No. 3 (March 1964), table 1, p. 356. States used in these calculations were: Alabama, Arkansas, Florida, Georgia, Kentucky, Louisiana, Maryland, Mississippi, North Carolina, Oklahoma, South Carolina, Tennessee, Texas, and Virginia.

[22] *1959 Agriculture Census,* vol. II, ch. X, table 7, pp. 1034–1035.

[23] *Ibid.*

[24] *Id.,* table 5, pp. 1032–1033, and table 7, pp. 1034–1035.

[25] Secretary Orville L. Freeman stated: "On the average, under today's conditions, gross sales of $10,000 or more are required for an adequate family farm operation . . . on the average, $10,000 gross sales is a useful figure for measuring adequate and inadequate farms." Statement of Secretary, U.S. Congress, House, Subcommittee of the Committee on Agriculture, *Hearings, The Family Farm,* 88th Cong., 1st Sess. (Serial P), July 11, 1963, Washington, D.C., p. 141.

farmers.[26] The special character of Southern agriculture may enable a farmer to obtain a sufficient livelihood from a lower value of farm products sold than the national estimate. If "marginally" viable farms are counted, 8.9 percent of the Negro farms and 26.2 percent of the white farms in the South could be considered adequate or potentially adequate.[27] Among commercial farmers in 1959,[28] the average value of products sold by Southern Negro farmers was $3,029; by white farmers, $10,396.[29]

The relative disadvantage of the Negro farm family is growing by other measures also. The disparity in income between white and Negro farm people increased between 1949 and 1959, and even by 1959, Negro income had not reached the 1949 income level for whites.

Median income—Rural farm families for the South [30]

	1949	*1959*
White	$1,366	$2,802
Nonwhite	712	1,259
Difference	654	1,543
Nonwhite as percent of White	52	45

[26] The Bureau of the Census has established six economic classes of commercial farms based on total value of all farm products sold. Percentages cited were obtained by adding all farms in economic classes I ($40,000 and over), II ($20,000 to $39,999), and III ($10,000 to $19,999) for the Southern States and dividing total into total number of farms. *1959 Agriculture Census,* vol. I, State table 17 for the Southern States (except the District of Columbia).

[27] Percentages based on economic classes I, II, III, and IV ($5,000 to $9,999) for the Southern States (except the District of Columbia).

[28] The Bureau of the Census defines "commercial" farms as those with a value of sales amounting to $2,500 or more, and those with a value of sales of $50 to $2,499 if the farm operator was under 65 years of age and (1) he did not work off the farm 100 days or more during the year and (2) the income received by the operator and members of his family from nonfarm sources was less than the value of farm products sold. *1959 Agriculture Census,* vol. II, p. xxxv. Of commercial farms 51 percent of those managed by Negroes sold less than $2,500 worth of farm products in 1959. For whites the percentage was 21.9. *1959 Agriculture Census,* vol. II, ch. X, p. 1030.

[29] *Ibid.*

[30] J. D. Cowhig and C. L. Beale, "Relative Socio-economic Status of Southern Whites and Nonwhites, 1950 and 1960," *The Southwestern Social Science Quarterly* (September 1964), table 3, p. 120. For States used in these calculations see note 21 *supra.* Dollar income unadjusted.

The disparity in education between Negro and white young adults was also growing, with Negroes still below the level of education enjoyed by whites a decade earlier.

Education—Percent of rural farm youth (25–29 years) with 12 or more years of school for the South [31]

	1950	*1960*
White	24.3	43.8
Nonwhite	7.0	15.8
Difference	17.3	28.0

A level of living index composed of varied and sensitive measures for 14 Southern States provides further evidence of the increasingly unequal status of the two groups. The absolute gap between the white and Negro levels of living indices nearly doubled from 1950 to 1959.

Level of living index—farm operators 14 State average [32]

	1950	*1959*
White	43	89
Nonwhite	19	46
Difference	24	43

The decrease in the number of Negro farm families living in crowded housing conditions was slight, while there were substantial improvements among white farm families. The percent of Negro farm homes with crowding in 1960 was still much greater than for whites 10 years earlier and the disparity between white and Negro farm households increased.

Percent of rural farm housing units with 1.01 or more persons per room for the South [33]

	1950	*1960*
White	25.8	14.6
Nonwhite	47.6	44.4
Difference	21.8	29.8

[31] *Ibid.*

[32] Cowhig and Beale, *Social Forces, op. cit.*, p. 357. For States and measures used in these calculations see note 21, *supra*.

[33] Cowhig and Beale, *Southwestern Social Science Quarterly, op. cit.*, table 3, p. 121.

Between 1950 and 1960 the gap between white and Negro farm families having hot and cold piped water in the home almost tripled.

Percent of rural farm housing units with hot and cold piped water for the South [34]

	1950	*1960*
White	20.4	60.0
Nonwhite	2.3	9.7
Difference	18.1	50.3

Thus, the overwhelming majority of Negro farm homes still lacked modern toilet, bathing, and kitchen facilities. In 1960, while 30 percent of Negro farm homes were dilapidated or deteriorating, only 7 percent of white farm homes were in that condition.[35]

RURAL NONFARM POPULATION

There were 3.2 million Negroes and 13.5 million whites living as nonfarm residents in rural areas of the South in 1960.[36] Sharp differences in socio-economic status were evident also between these Negroes and their white counterparts. The position of the rural nonfarm Negro was somewhat better than that of the Negro who remained on the farm. But he was at a considerable disadvantage relative to white rural nonfarm residents, as shown in the following tables.

The difference in income between white and Negro rural nonfarm families nearly doubled between 1949 and 1959. The proportion of Negro nonfarm families living in crowded conditions remained unchanged during the decade, while for whites there was a decrease of one third. While a higher proportion of Negro rural nonfarm families had modern plumbing facilities in 1960, the margin by which whites led had considerably widened in the decade. By 1960 all but 7 percent of white rural nonfarm housing

[34] *Ibid.*

[35] *Ibid.*

[36] *1960 Census of Population,* PC(2)–1C, Nonwhite Population by Race, table I, p. 1; *1960 Census of Population,* PC(1)–1C, U.S. Summary, table 107, p. 258.

was in sound condition, but one third of Negro rural nonfarm homes were dilapidated or deteriorating.

Only in education did the gap between Negroes and whites remain constant, although by 1960 Negroes still had not achieved the 1950 educational level of whites.

Disparities between white and nonwhite rural nonfarm families for the South, 1950–60 [37]

Education—percent of youth (25–29 yrs.) with 12 or more years of school

	1950	1960
White	36.1	47.7
Nonwhite	11.2	22.8
Difference	24.9	24.9

Median income—Dollars

	1949	1959
White	1,944	3,504
Nonwhite	895	1,529
Difference	1,049	1,975
Nonwhite as percent of white	46	44

Percent of housing units with hot and cold piped water in the house

	1950	1960
White	41.0	63.6
Nonwhite	5.4	15.9
Difference	35.6	47.7

Percent of housing units with 1.01 or more persons per room

	1950	1960
White	24.3	16.6
Nonwhite	36.9	36.9
Difference	12.6	20.3

Percent of housing units in unsound condition

	1950	1960
White	15.2	7.3
Nonwhite	44.3	32.7
Difference	29.1	25.4

CHANGING POPULATION OF THE RURAL SOUTH

Wars, industrialization, urbanization, and mechanization have contributed to drastic decline in farm population and large scale population shifts.[38] The rate of urbanization of the Negroes in the last 50 years has surpassed even that of whites.[39] Between 1935

[37] Cowhig and Beale, *Southwestern Social Science Quarterly, op. cit.*, table 3, pp. 120–121. For States used in these calculations see note 21, *supra.*

[38] U.S. Department of Labor, *Manpower Report of the President and a Report on Manpower Requirements, Resources, Utilization, and Training* (March 1964), pp. 80–81.

[39] In 1960, 69.8 percent of U.S. population was urban. Among Negroes the rate was 72.4 percent. Weaver, Robert C., *The Urban Complex: Human Values in Urban Life* (Garden City: Doubleday & Co., Inc., 1964), pp. 229–30.

and 1959 the number of white Southern farmers dropped from 2.6 million to 1.4 million. Nonwhite Southern farmers declined from 816,000 to 266,000 in the same period.[40]

An important feature of the decline of the Southern farm population has been the changing patterns of land tenure. A large part of the decline in farm population has been among the tenants, due to the drastic decline in the need for manual labor on the large cotton plantations.[41] In the 25 years between 1935 and 1959 the number of tenants dropped by over 70 percent.[42]

This movement of white and Negro population from the farms of the South will undoubtedly continue. However, many Negroes displaced from the farms have remained in the rural areas of the South. The 1.5 million Negroes in farm families and the 3.2 million rural nonfarm Negroes of the South comprise a major element in the arc of poverty which sweeps from Maryland to Texas—the largest geographic and social concentration of the poor. This is seen clearly in the maps on the following page.

The Secretary of Agriculture has described the Department's responsibilities as extending to both the farm and nonfarm families:[43]

> Today there is a substantial number of family farms which are not adequate in terms of gross marketings. Our goal is to enable them to become adequate, efficient family farms or to help the families who live on them to find either adequate nonfarm rural employment or, if they choose, opportunities for jobs outside their present community.

The effectiveness of the programs of the Department of Agriculture in raising the social, economic, and educational level of Negro residents of the rural South is of prime importance to citizens in all parts of our Nation. Many of these disadvantaged families move to the urban centers of both the North and the

[40] *1959 Agriculture Census,* vol. II, ch. X, table 5, pp. 1032–1033. Figures rounded to nearest thousand in this report.

[41] Population Reference Bureau, *op. cit.,* pp. 63, 73–74.

[42] *1959 Agriculture Census,* vol. II, ch. X, table 5, pp. 1032–1033.

[43] Statement by Secretary Orville L. Freeman, *The Family Farm,* p. 141.

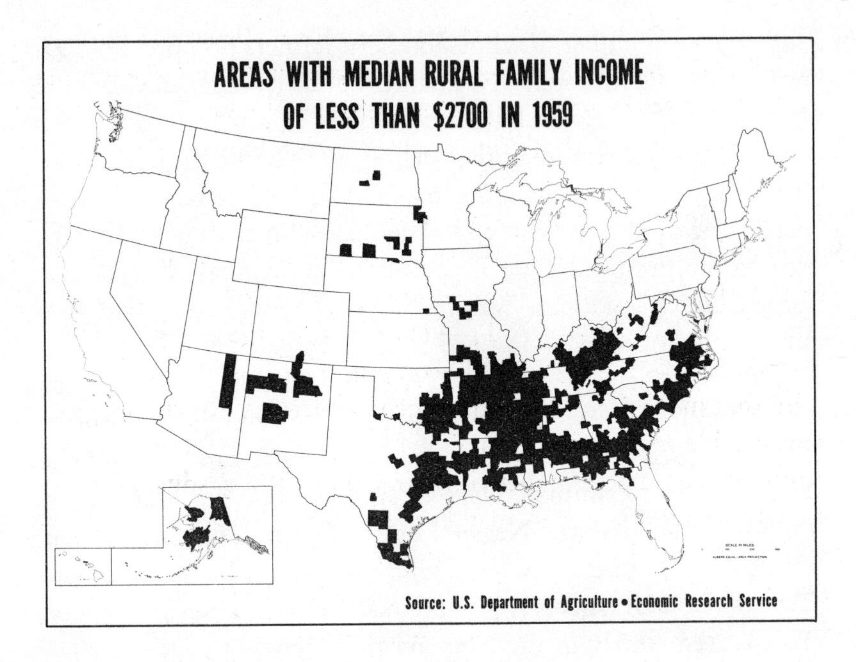
AREAS WITH MEDIAN RURAL FAMILY INCOME
OF LESS THAN $2700 IN 1959
Source: U.S. Department of Agriculture • Economic Research Service

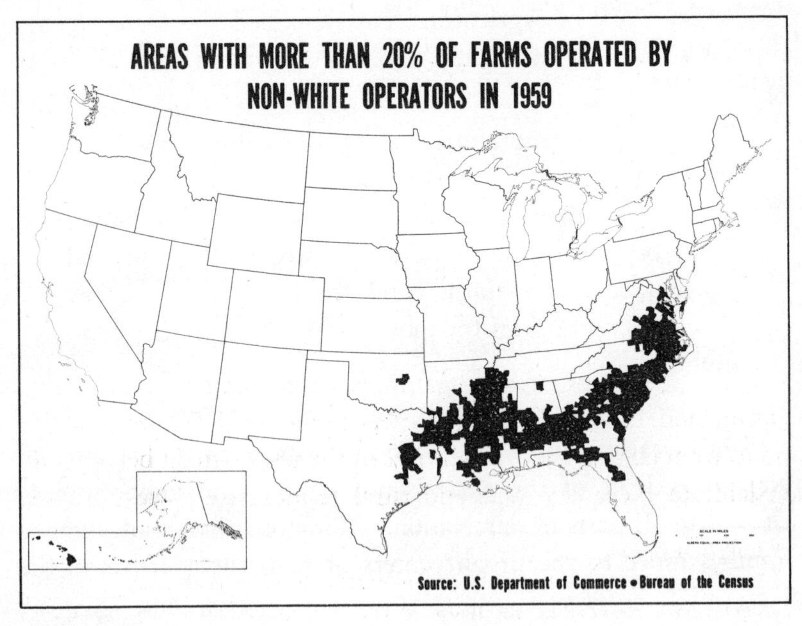
AREAS WITH MORE THAN 20% OF FARMS OPERATED BY
NON-WHITE OPERATORS IN 1959
Source: U.S. Department of Commerce • Bureau of the Census

South where they find the demand for their unskilled and semi-skilled labor rapidly decreasing.[44] Cities outside the South share the cost in human waste which too often results when these migrants join the ranks of the chronically unemployed and disoriented.

As for the South itself, its rate of growth and development, the pace of its industrial expansion, its hope for prosperity in both its rural and urban areas will depend in large measure on the capacity of its 4.7 million Negro rural residents to make the fullest possible contribution to the social and economic progress of the region.

In the analysis of the Department programs which follows, considerable attention is given to evidences of inequities of opportunity and treatment in activities and programs conducted on a racially separate basis. It may be well to note here that the Department's programs have been studied in the light of long standing Federal policy against discrimination based on race in direct Federal programs. Racial discrimination in the recruitment, employment, training and promotion of employees by the Federal Government has been prohibited by Presidential directive for over twenty years.[45] In 1954 the Supreme Court issued the first of a series of decisions declaring "separate but equal" public facilities and institutions unconstitutional.[46] The enactment of Title VI of the Civil Rights Act of 1964,[47] prohibiting discrimination under any program receiving Federal financial assistance, further clarified the role of the Federal Government in actively promoting equal protection of the laws in federally aided programs.

In attempting to measure the policies and practices of the Department of Agriculture against the foregoing standards, the Commission found certain questions particularly relevant: How and to what degree have the services of the Department been made available to Negro farmers and rural residents? Have Negroes

---

[44] *Manpower Report, op. cit.*, p. 5.

[45] Exec. Order No. 9980, 13 Fed. Reg. 4311 (1948); Exec. Order No. 10590, 20 Fed. Reg. 409 (1955); Exec. Order No. 10925, 26 Fed. Reg. 1977 (1961); Exec. Order No. 11114, 28 Fed. Reg. 6485 (1963)

[46] *Brown* v. *Board of Education*, 347 U.S. 483 (1954).

[47] P.L. 88–352, 78 Stat. 241 (1964).

participated with whites in decision-making processes at the State and local levels? Have Federal programs to encourage crop diversification, soil conservation practices, and improved farm and money management been administered equally for Negroes and whites?

The answers to these questions provide valuable information for the evaluation of current programs affecting both races, as well as for the formulation of new programs to deal with the special problems of rural poverty. For as President Johnson has stated: [48]

> We must give as much time and attention to low-income people on farms and in rural areas as we have given to commodities for the past 30 years.

---

[48] President Lyndon B. Johnson's answer to question in "Where I Stand on Farming," *The Farm Journal,* October 1964, p. 56.

II. THE COOPERATIVE EXTENSION SERVICE

The Cooperative Extension Service is the educational arm of the Department of Agriculture. The purpose of this chapter is to identify the ways in which this Federal-State program has used its particular skills to serve the Negro farmers of the South.

Education has been the key in the change from the old to the new in agriculture and it remains the key today. The introduction of new methods of farming has been part of a continuing program sponsored by the Federal Government since 1862, when Congress created the Department of Agriculture to acquire and diffuse information and established land-grant colleges to teach agriculture and mechanic arts.[1] These colleges were outgrowths of the earlier farmers' institutes which began in 1853.[2] Later, in the 1880's, agricultural research stations were established through Congressional action at most land-grant colleges.[3] At the turn of the century, trains were used as mobile classrooms to bring agricultural knowledge from the colleges to the farmers.[4] By 1904 the Department of Agriculture was sending "special agents" to fight the boll weevil in the South. Later the practice of assigning such agents was extended to other parts of the country in response to other pressing needs of American farmers.[5]

Agricultural extension work was formalized in 1914 by the

---

[1] 12 Stat. 387 (1862), 5 U.S.C. 511; The First Morrill Act, 12 Stat. 503 (1862), 7 U.S.C. 301.

[2] True, Alfred Charles, *A History of Agricultural Extension Work, 1785–1923* (Washington: U.S. Government Printing Office, 1928), p. 5.

[3] Pursuant to the Hatch Act, 24 Stat. 440 (1887), and others, 7 U.S.C. 361a.

[4] True, *op. cit.*, p. 28ff

[5] USDA, *Century of Service: the First Hundred Years* (Washington: U.S. Government Printing Office, 1963), pp. 43–44.

Smith-Lever Act as a function of the land-grant colleges in cooperation with the Department "to aid in diffusing among the people of the United States useful and practical information on subjects relating to agriculture and home economics, and to encourage the application of same." [6]

From these beginnings a vast educational system has developed on the local level, radiating out of the land-grant colleges, linking the county and its problems to the expertise of the colleges' academic departments.

While its first responsibility continues to be service to farmers, in recent years the Extension Service has been called upon to provide more generalized educational assistance to a much broader clientele, including nonfarm rural residents and urban residents. Increased recognition of the plight of low-income families has led the Extension Service to re-emphasize that its primary objective is to help "people overcome the obstacles that stand in the way of their progress." [7] It has been largely through the Extension program that the Department of Agriculture has sought to improve the social and economic status of impoverished Southern rural residents.

ADMINISTRATIVE STRUCTURE

Generally

The Federal Extension Service (FES) provides national leadership to the States in developing their agricultural programs, and encourages State extension workers to try new paths and learn from the experience of others. FES helps train State extension workers and in addition evaluates programs.[8]

---

[6] 38 Stat. 372 (1914), as amended, 7 U.S.C. 341.

[7] U.S. Congress, House, Subcommittee of Committee on Appropriations, *Hearings on Department of Agriculture Appropriations*, 1964, 88th Cong., 1st Sess., pt. 2, Statement of Administrator p. 859 (hereinafter referred to as *1964 Appropriations Hearings*).

[8] *1964 Appropriations Hearings*, pt. 2, p. 863.

Funds are allocated by Congress among the States on a formula basis determined primarily by a State's percentage of the rural and farm population of the United States. The extent of Federal financial assistance to the Southern States for cooperative agricultural extension work is significant. Eleven Southern States received $24.3 million or 33 percent of Federal extension funds allotted to the States for fiscal year 1964. The Federal share of total funds expended for extension work within these States ranged from a low of 23 percent in Florida to 55 percent in South Carolina. For the 11 States, the average Federal contribution was 41.5 percent.[9]

At the State level, the State extension service as a unit of the land-grant colleges operates with the advice and assistance of the Federal Extension Service. It is responsible for supervising and directing all extension work in the State as well as for formulating and organizing statewide programs.[10] The State office staff typically includes a director, whose appointment is subject to the approval of the USDA, and assistants, program planners, area or district supervisors, subject-matter specialists, and management personnel.[11]

The State extension services have developed cooperative financing and administration with the county governments, "thus placing an important part of the responsibility for planning, financing, and conducting work in each of the counties, even closer to the people." [12] This responsibility extends to priorities of work, allocation of time and resources, and assignment of staff.[13]

---

[9] *1965 Appropriations Hearings,* pt. 2, p. 364. For details of funds see app. A.

[10] Memorandum of Understanding Between Land-Grant Institution and the U.S.D.A. on Cooperative Extension Work in Agriculture and Home Economics *1965 Appropriations Hearings,* pt. 2, pp. 382–384.

[11] USDA FES files, State Annual Plans of Work; *County Agents Directory 1964.* (Chicago: C. L. Mast, Jr. & Associates, 1964.)

[12] Statement of Administrator, *1965 Appropriations Hearings,* pt. 2, p. 367; Gladys Baker, *The County Agent, Studies in Public Administration,* vol. XI (Chicago: University of Chicago Press, 1939), p. 127.

[13] USDA, FES, Extension Committee on Organization and Policy, *The Cooperative Extension Service Today, a Statement of Scope and Responsibility* (Washington, 1958), p. 13. Hereinafter cited as *Scope Report 1958.*

Personnel of the State extension service working at the county level, usually known as county agents and home demonstration agents, are responsible for supplying information to residents at the local level. Subject-matter specialists from the land-grant college make county visits to advise agents on particular problems and assist farmers in their special field of competence. Agents usually specialize in agricultural subjects, such as crops or livestock, in 4-H clubs, and in home demonstration.

Activities of the county agents include visiting farms and advising individual farmers; organizing and serving 4-H and home demonstration clubs as well as associations and cooperatives; arranging demonstrations, farmers' classes, and lectures by specialists; assisting in community development committees; conducting tours of experiment stations; using daily radio programs, regular newspaper columns, and TV appearances to disseminate information to farmers on other Department programs; and assisting other agricultural agencies in setting program goals. They are assisted by an advisory committee of local residents selected by the county agent, frequently with the advice of local producers associations, county officials, the school board, and other interested groups and individuals.[14] The advisory committee draws up a county plan of work under which the county extension staff functions.

In the South

In the South, State extension services have devised a separate and segregated structure of service for the Negro farmer and his family who are served primarily by Negro Extension workers. The Smith-Lever Act,[15] creating the Cooperative Extension Service, allowed those State legislatures which had established segregated land-grant colleges under the Second Morrill Act of 1890[16] to designate either the white or the Negro college to administer the program of agricultural extension work. An attempt to amend

[14] For an earlier description see Baker, *op. cit.*, p. 133.

[15] 38 Stat. 372, 373 (1914), 7 U.S.C. 341.

[16] 26 Stat. 417, 418 (1890), 7 U.S.C. 323.

the bill to include a specific requirement that extension work among Negroes be carried out at the Negro land-grant colleges was defeated upon the ground, among others, that divided responsibility for the use of extension funds in a State might lead to "dissimilar instruction being given to white and negro [sic] farmers."[17] In the 17 States with segregated institutions[18] the white land-grant college was chosen to administer the total program.[19] However, as the Southern extension services employed Negro State and district leaders in the ensuing years, these men were generally placed in the Negro land-grant colleges.[20] Since that time federally-supported State extension services in the South have been operated on a segregated structural basis at both State and county levels.

In 11 Southern States where most rural Negroes live, the Commission found that extension work at the State level was carried on by two separate staffs, one for white and one for Negro work, operating from two headquarters, with frequently overlapping jurisdictions. In Florida, Louisiana, and Tennessee organizational structure placed responsibility for the supervision of Negro extension workers in the white state office. In Louisiana, Negro state staff, in a separate office, was described by the white officials as functioning in the same manner as the white District program specialists, except covering the whole state. In other states two separate administrative structures formulated and implemented the Negro and white programs.

Of these States, ten maintained the State director of extension and his white staff at the formerly all-white land-grant colleges and a Negro State staff at another location, usually the "Negro" land-grant college.[21] Administrative responsibility for work with

---

[17] True, *op. cit.*, p. 114.

[18] Alabama, Arkansas, Delaware, Florida, Georgia, Kentucky, Louisiana, Maryland, Mississippi, Missouri, North Carolina, Oklahoma, South Carolina, Tennessee, Texas, Virginia, West Virginia. United States Commission on Civil Rights, *Equal Protection of the Laws in Public Higher Education* (Washington: U.S. Government Printing Office, 1960), p. 278.

[19] Baker, *op. cit.*, p. 195.

[20] True, *op. cit.*, p. 190.

[21] For a listing of the white and Negro State extension offices in Southern States see app. B.

Negroes was found to be divided between the white and Negro offices. Thus, instances were found where the Negro State leader was responsible for the programming function for Negro home demonstration work, but the white director (or specialist) was responsible for the budget function; training was handled separately while other personnel functions were centralized; geographic boundaries for administrative purposes were different for white and Negro staff.

County Office Facilities.—In 11 Southern States the segregated structure of the State Extension Service persisted down to the local level where separate and unequal county offices are maintained for white and Negro staff. The Commission found that the Extension tradition of having the location of offices determined at the county level has generally operated to enforce racial segregation and perpetuate gross inequities in the South. White extension service officials took little responsibility for the provision of suitable office space for Negro extension workers. Thus, in one Alabama county, when the white extension staff moved into the new county courthouse the Negro agent asked the white county agent about obtaining space for his office and was told to see the county judge. The judge advised him that no provision had been made to house the Negro staff.

Supervision.—Lines of authority and supervision for Negro county workers were frequently unclear. In Louisiana, Mississippi, and North Carolina the State officials said that the county agent was responsible for coordinating the entire extension program within his county and for the supervision of Negro agents, if any, assigned to his county. However, in two States, the lack of supervision of the Negro worker at the county level was open and recognized.

In Alabama white county agents stated that they were not the supervisors of Negro agents and disclaimed any responsibility for the Negro agents' work. The separation of white and Negro agents was so clear that Negro agents even had stencils cut at the Negro State extension headquarters at Tuskegee, although the white staff had a full complement of stenographic workers available to do the work in the same county.

In Virginia Negro agents were not responsible to white county agents, although the State office said it "tries to arrange for collaboration and exchange of material."

In Georgia the situation was confused, with one white county agent asserting that he was the supervisor of the Negro assistant agent, while the latter believed that he was responsible to the Negro State staff.

Although South Carolina State officials considered that Negro workers were supervised by white agents, on the county level Negro workers were uncertain to whom they were responsible. One Negro assistant agent thought that his supervisor was the Negro statewide assistant in Agricultural Extension, but that his reports were "censored" by the white county agent. Another gave the impression that he was free to work on his own without obtaining clearance from the county agent.

THE SEGREGATED STRUCTURE IN OPERATION

State Staff and Statewide Meetings

The Commission found that the physical isolation of the Negro worker excluded him from the flow of much of the information which he was supposed to transmit to rural and farm families. This isolation began at the top of the segregated structure with the inequality between the educational facilities to which Negro and white workers were assigned. The white State staffs were located at major educational institutions which included Experiment Stations and a full complement of research and teaching staffs where there were daily contacts with a wide range of disciplines. The Negro State staff were located at Negro land-grant colleges which were generally poor, limited in scope, and deficient in staff and equipment.[22] Only in Texas did the Negro extension

[22] For a discussion of conditions in Negro land-grant colleges, see Edward D. Eddy, Jr., *Colleges for Our Land and Time* (New York: Harper & Bros., 1956), chap. 8, "The Negro Land-Grant College," esp. pp. 163–165; and West Virginia State College Bulletin Series 21, No. 5, *Land-Grant Colleges for Negroes* by John W. Davis (April 1934), *passim.*

761–685 O—65——3

staff have access to an on-campus Experiment Station—a substation of the larger scientific unit in the white college. While agricultural research grants from USDA constituted an important source of support of the white land-grant college, creating a scientific community which included the white extension staff, the Negro land-grant colleges received little in the way of Federal funds for research. For example, allotments to white land-grant colleges in the States of Alabama, Arkansas, Florida, Georgia, Louisiana, Mississippi, North Carolina, South Carolina, Tennessee, Texas, and Virginia made by the Cooperative State Research Service in 1964 totaled $11,640,000. Negro land-grant colleges in those States received no allotments from CSRS in the same period.[23]

At the State offices of the extension service for the white staff there were staff members specializing in a wide variety of subject-matter areas—ranging from 43 subjects in Texas to about 20 in some other States. Except for North Carolina, the Negro State staff included no specialists trained in commodities or agricultural technology.[24] This inequality has long been noted. An earlier commentator stated that a few Negro State staff members were called "specialists," "although instead of one subject-matter field they are responsible for many."[25] The separately housed Negro State staff were thus deprived of the informal contacts with agricultural scientists regarded by the Department as a valuable aid to staff members in their role as extension educators.

Joint meetings of Negro and white State staffs might overcome some of this disadvantage. However, only North Carolina, Mississippi, and Texas reported monthly staff contact between Negro and white State extension staff. In other States contact was minimal. In Alabama, Negro and white State staffs met jointly once a year. In South Carolina and Virginia the staffs met separately.

[23] *Letter from USDA to Commission on Civil Rights,* Jan. 4, 1965.

[24] In Arkansas and Texas there are Negro personnel doing Farm and Home Development work. West Virginia employs a Negro female in Family Life and Human Relations.

[25] Baker, *op. cit.*, p. 196. Only Alabama and North Carolina were noted as having Negro specialists in 1939.

Negroes attended only those occasional meetings to which they were invited.

The importance of these staff meetings is illustrated by one incident which occurred in Louisiana. On the agenda of one meeting was the making of plans for two area Economic Development Conferences. These conferences were considered so important that the Secretary of Agriculture commented on the launching of the Louisiana program in his Annual Report, stating that its purpose was "to stimulate thinking, planning and constructive action by local people." [26] However, Negro staff were not invited to the planning sessions or the conferences.

A 1928 history of extension work described annual regional conferences attended by both Negro and white extension personnel.[27] The Commission staff found no comparable regional contact between Negro and white State extension workers in 1964.

The annual or biennial statewide staff meetings of the Extension Service are also occasions for the transmission of specialized knowledge and information on other programs of the Department of Agriculture. However, segregation again interferes with and obstructs the flow of vitally needed information. Except in Arkansas, Florida, North Carolina, and Texas, these meetings were held separately. For instance,[28] in 1963 when the Mississippi Extension Service celebrated its 50th anniversary in Jackson, the white staff met at a downtown hotel, the Negro staff at College Park Auditorium. Both programs were entitled "50 Years of Extension Progress . . . Now What?" Four white speakers delivered identical speeches at different times to the white and Negro meetings, one on "Mississippi in the Space Age." The white agents were also addressed by the State directors of three Federal agencies in the State—Farmers Home Administration, Soil Conservation Service, and Agricultural Stabilization and Conservation Service—as well

---

[26] United States Department of Agriculture, *Report of the Secretary of Agriculture, 1963* (Washington, D.C., 1964), p. 17.

[27] True, *op. cit.*, p. 190.

[28] Information on the segregated State extension conferences discussed below is taken from the official programs of each conference. Copies are retained in Commission files.

as by the director of the State Employment Security Commission. The Negro meeting was addressed by the Negro program staff assistant of the Farmers Home Administration. Other Federal programs were not presented.

In Alabama in 1964, the separate annual conferences of the white and Negro extension staff had the Federal Extension Service administrator giving the same speech in different parts of the State to separate audiences on successive days. While both conferences had a symposium on "Serving Alabama's Changing Audiences," the white panel was headed by two State specialists, while the Negro panel had no specialists at all.

Louisiana held a statewide meeting to celebrate its 50th Anniversary of Extension on August 3, 1964. The traditional form of separation was observed with a ceremony at the formerly all-white land-grant college (which was under a court order to desegregate) in the morning and a ceremony at the Negro land-grant college in the same city in the evening. Even though the Secretary of Agriculture, pursuant to a White House instruction, had issued a directive that Federal officials should not address segregated meetings,[29] one Federal Extension Service official addressed the white section of the Louisiana meeting by long distance telephone.

County Staff

Segregated and Unequal Offices.—Negro county staff were usually in segregated offices, and the contrast between white and Negro offices in most Southern counties was striking. Negro offices were most often found in inferior buildings where the space, furnishings of the office, supplies, and supportive services were inadequate and lower in quality and quantity than those provided the white staff. In some cases segregated offices were even found in Federal buildings. The overall situation found by the Commission in 1964 represented some improvement over the findings recorded in a 1939 study of county agents, which noted that Negro county

[29] USDA, Memo from Office of the Secretary to Assistant Secretaries, Agency Heads, and Staff Assistants, June 23, 1964. For text see app. C.

agents did not have offices or clerical assistance and usually worked out of their homes.[30] A comparison of white and Negro offices in counties visited by Commission staff showed, however:

Gross disparities in size of offices and/or physical condition;

White offices in Federal or Post Office building; Negro offices in private structures;[31]

White offices with air conditioning and Negro offices without air conditioning or fans and heated only by portable heaters.

Where white offices were fully equipped and staffed, the Commission found:

Negro offices without telephones;

Negro offices without electricity;

Negro offices with part-time or no secretarial services; no janitorial services;

Negro offices without typewriter or office supplies and with inferior office equipment.

Not only were typewriters frequently not available to Negro agents, but one agent in Alabama reported he purchased a mimeograph machine with his own money.

Although Extension officials recognized that the operation of the extension service in a county would be more efficient if white and Negro personnel were located together, until the issuance of Department of Agriculture regulations pursuant to Title VI of the Civil Rights Act of 1964,[32] there were no Federal or State policies prohibiting the maintenance of racially segregated offices.

Segregated Staff Meetings.—At the county level the frequent exclusion of Negro agents from regular staff meetings where white agents discussed problems, made plans, coordinated activities, and reached decisions affecting the whole county emphasized the sepa-

---

[30] Baker, *op. cit.*, p. 197.

[31] A notable example of such disparity was found in Sumter County, Ala., where the white office was located in a Federal building and the Negro office was located over a pool hall.

[32] 7 CFR 15.1 *et seq.*, Dec. 4, 1964.

ration of the two staffs. Thus, Negro staff were further isolated from the main sources of information and assistance.

A white county agent in Alabama stated that weekly staff meetings were not attended by the Negro agent. A Negro agent in another Alabama county reported that while he met occasionally with the county agent, no formal schedule of meetings was established and he did not meet with other white staff.

In one parish in Louisiana a Negro home demonstration worker reported that she had monthly meetings with her white counterpart but that she was excluded from the regular weekly staff meetings. If she happened to come to the office while such a meeting was in progress she was asked to come back later. In Mississippi the pattern of separate staff meetings also prevailed. In one county white and Negro staff meetings were held separately, though the county agent himself met with Negro staff every other month or in connection with a particular problem. In a South Carolina county where the white agent reported that the white staff met "practically every morning," the Negro staff was said to attend these meetings only "at times . . . if something pertains to them." Only in two Georgia counties visited did the Commission find Negro county workers attending regular meetings of extension staff.

When the Rural Areas Development (RAD) program, designed to attack chronic unemployment and other economic problems, was organized, the segregated structure of extension again interfered with the communication of information to Negroes. In one South Carolina county for example, Negro workers were not invited to extension staff meetings to learn of this Federal activity. The white county agent did not discuss RAD with the Negro agent until approximately one year after the program had been established. At this time the Negro agent was told in vague terms "to work through the State system."

Segregated Training.—The State extension services provide numerous opportunities for county extension workers to raise their professional competence and improve their work effectiveness through in-service and academic training.

These training opportunities are vital to the effectiveness of the county agent and the economic welfare of the farmers he serves. They provide new and timely information on developments in the various fields of agriculture, farming, and rural life, add to the agent's professional skill, and serve as an important means of communication within the extension service. Since Negro agents have come largely from the inferior segregated school systems of the South they could have benefitted most from these training opportunities.

While there is considerable variation in quality and quantity of training among the various States, consistent and clear disparities were found between training for white and Negro workers in 13 Southern States for which data was studied.[33] Only in North Carolina were county agents trained on a desegregated basis. In general, in the remaining 12 States, training of extension agents was segregated, and training available to white workers was more varied, longer, and more detailed than that available to Negro workers.

In Georgia Negro county agents were offered only two courses while white agents received training in 13 subjects. In Mississippi Negro county agents received no training in cotton or pasture and forage although whites did. In Texas Negro county agents received no training in livestock, although white agents were offered two 5-day livestock workshops and a 5-day marketing school.

In Arkansas Negro county agents received no training in livestock or poultry or related matters, while white county agents received training in dairying, poultry, beef cattle, swine, and forage crops. In Louisiana white male agents were trained in eight 4–H subjects by many State specialists, averaging 4½ days per worker. Negro men received one 4–H training course on "organization" from two district program specialists, or 1 day of training per worker. White home demonstration workers also received

[33] The information in this discussion is based on schedules of training for 1963 and 1964 submitted to the FES by the State Cooperative Extension Services as well as field interviews by Commission staff. Copies of training schedules are retained in Commission files.

training in eight 4-H subject-matter areas, while the Negro women workers received no 4-H training. In South Carolina training for home demonstration workers followed the same pattern.[34]

Subject matter and content of courses for Negro workers is frequently limited, and training tends to be general rather than specific. In general, less time is devoted to each subject for Negroes than for whites, and consequently subjects are treated with less depth and scope. For instance, in Georgia all livestock training was combined in a single 1-day meeting for Negro county agents, while whites had three meetings on various aspects of the subject. In Virginia Negro agents attended a 2-day meeting covering tobacco, peanuts, soybeans, weeds, and fertilizers. White agents had a two-week training course of flue-cured tobacco production and marketing alone, as well as other meetings on tobacco and six different meetings on peanut diseases. Similar disparities in training prevailed for Negro and white home demonstration agents in Arkansas and Georgia.[35]

Important differences in the timing of training meetings work to the disadvantage of Negro agents. For example, in Alabama in January 1964 white agents received 2 days of cotton training well before the beginning of the cotton planting season. Negro agents covered the same subject in a half day in April. A Negro agent reported that since cotton was planted about March 25, the April meeting was too late to be useful that year. A similar situation existed in Arkansas. White agents attended a meeting on

---

[34] In South Carolina, where training for all workers was less than in other States, Negro home demonstration agents received no subject-matter training, but white home demonstration agents were trained in home management and clothing, in addition to the information received at their annual conference.

[35] In Arkansas three different training sessions of 2-day duration were held for white home demonstration agents on economics of family living, human relations, and time management with an additional day on family relations. Negro home demonstration agents training was limited to a 1-day meeting on home management and a half day each for family living and county development. In Georgia, Negro home demonstration agents attended a 2-day meeting on family life with an agenda covering six areas. White home demonstration agents had separate meetings of from 1 to 4 days devoted to each of 11 subjects.

cotton in late January, while Negro county agents had a cotton meeting in the same city late in March.

Generally, it appeared that Negro agents were given in-service training only in subject areas in which Negro farmers and rural population were already deeply involved, such as cotton and other row crops, manual skills, and subsistence living. One State program was directed toward training Negro agents "within the context of the role expectations held for them by society."

Besides in-service training, the Extension Services cooperate with State universities and colleges in providing regular summer sessions particularly oriented toward graduate degrees in agricultural education. Until recently, such training was not available to Negro agents in the southern schools attended by white agents. As late as the summer of 1964 Negro county agents from several States gathered for training at Negro schools.[36]

While Negro agents attended one class at the Louisiana State University campus for the first time in the summer of 1964 they were segregated from white extension workers. Negro agents in Louisiana were notified by the State extension service that they could enroll in one graduate course at the formerly all white Louisiana State University. However, they were sent a separate notice telling them which section of the course to attend. White agents, by specific instruction from the Louisiana extension service, attended another section of the same course.[37] Furthermore, a course on 4-H programs required for a Masters Degree in Agricultural Extension Education was not open to Negro agents.

Visits of State subject-matter specialists with county agents are another form of training. These visits are made at the request of the county agents or on the initiative of the specialist and sometimes at the request of an individual farmer or a farmers' association. They serve to acquaint the county agents and farmers with the most recent research developments and with the experiences of other farmers in dealing with similar problems.

---

[36] Prairie View A & M in Texas and Tuskegee Institute, Ala.

[37] Memo from State Extension Official to "Assistant Agents for Work With Negroes," Feb. 27, 1964, and to "Selected Extension Personnel," Feb. 27, 1964; copies retained in Commission files.

Because of the segregated structure of the service, Negro agents have not had the same opportunities as white agents to benefit from the subject-matter specialists. Twenty-five years ago a study of the extension service indicated that in some States white specialists were required to notify the Negro agent of their impending visit to his county. At that time, the study noted that "the Negro county agent is usually allowed to attend" meetings with specialists.[38] Field investigations by the Commission staff showed that this is no longer the case. In counties dispersed through a number of States Negro agents were not present at, or invited to, meetings which the State specialist had with white staff and white farmers.

Thus, in Alabama a white county agent advised that in the spring of 1964 specialists had visited the county on six occasions to discuss cotton, seed drying, landscaping, soybeans, and forage. No Negro staff were present at any meeting.[39]

In Georgia Negro agents met with the commodity specialists only if Negroes were already producing the crop under discussion. According to a State extension official, if the county agent asked a specialist to come in and discuss greenhouse tomatoes with agents and tomato farmers, the Negro agent would not be asked to be present because Negroes currently were not in that crop. In Louisiana a white county agent stated that white specialists had visited the parish on 10 occasions during a 6-week period. The Negro workers did not meet with any of these specialists or any other specialists during this period. In Mississippi a Negro worker stated, "When white specialists have the time they will meet with Negro county agents." A South Carolina State official asserted that all agents participated equally in the services rendered by

---

[38] Baker, *op. cit.*, pp. 196–197.

[39] One county agent claimed that the Negro agent would be invited to meet with a specialist while in the county if they were to discuss "some particular phase that the Negro farmer is interested in." However, although several of the Negro farmers were cotton growers, the Negro agent was not invited to attend a meeting with a cotton specialist. Oher county agents confirmed they do not, as a matter of practice, invite Negro agents to specialists' meetings. One agent said he was occasionally instructed to inform the Negro agent of the specialist's visit.

specialists. However, a white county agent stated, "When [the Negro agent] finds something he can't handle, he comes here—whenever we find some things we can't handle, we call a specialist."

In North Carolina reasonable requests for specialists are said to be honored. However, it is the Negro State specialists who usually serve Negro agents. Since the orientation of the Negro specialists is more general than that of whites, the latter are available to assist their Negro colleagues if more particular knowledge is required.

In a county with a staff of several agents the usual procedure might be for only one agent to attend a meeting on a specialized subject and then to transmit the information to his fellow county workers. If the extension offices and services were integrated, the fact that a Negro agent did not attend meetings on specialized subjects could be explained by his position as one among several agents in a county. But in the existing extension structure the separately housed Negro staff is not, in fact, a functioning part of the county extension service and does not have the benefit of regular contact with the workers who have received training. In the absence of special efforts to overcome the obstacles of a segregated structure, the information acquired by white agents in training is of little benefit to Negro agents.

In addition to these formal and informal training opportunities available to the county extension staff, agents receive bulletins and publications from the State extension office, agricultural experiment stations, the Federal Extension Service, and other agencies of the Department of Agriculture. All serve to keep the county worker informed on aspects of county extension work and on related Federal programs. However, in one South Carolina county the difference in number of publications received by the white and Negro offices was surprising. The white agent provided Commission representatives with copies of 31 publications which he had received during the preceding months. The Negro assistant agent could list only seven publications which his separate office received during the same period.

Denied adequate training and cut off from vital information, Negro personnel were often found to be unfamiliar with programs of great importance to their communities. In some South Carolina and Georgia counties Negro personnel interviewed were unfamiliar with the Manpower Development and Training Act, although their white coworkers were informed on the subject.[40] In one Mississippi county, information on acreage allotments was provided by the ASCS office manager to the white county agent but not the Negro agent. The initial training for one Georgia Negro extension worker did not include information on the programs of the Farmers Home Administration in his county, and other Negro workers in Alabama, Georgia, Mississippi, and South Carolina were unfamiliar with the Rural Areas Development program.

Not only were Negro extension workers excluded from meetings with their fellow staff members, but in Alabama, Georgia, and Mississippi it was found that they did not participate in meetings with workers of other agricultural agencies in their counties. In one case this isolation was so complete that a Negro agent did not know and was not known to other agricultural workers in that county. A Federal Crop Insurance Corporation official in Georgia, who claimed that information concerning this program was made available to Negro extension staff, did not know that a Negro agent was employed in the county in which his own office was located.

Federal Responsibility.—The Federal Extension Service plays an important role in developing training materials and giving assistance to States in preparing in-service training programs. Frequently, FES staff teach in such educational programs within the State. It has been the practice of the FES to permit its officials to participate in segregated training meetings and to assist in planning for segregated training.

At the request of the Commission FES secured from State exten-

[40] MDTA establishes primarily a job training program for unemployed heads of household, and youth and farm workers with annual income less than $1,200. Training and expenses are paid for by the State and Federal governments. Institutional training may extend for 52 weeks and could include training for such farm positions as general farmer, farmhand, truck farmer, and dairy farmhand.

sion services reports of training offered to extension workers which served as the basis for the Commission's analysis. Throughout long discussions of the disparities revealed by this data, however, FES officials made no reference to any prior evaluation of the quality and quantity of training offered white and Negro extension workers.

Another FES activity with professional development as its goal is the Washington "Agricultural Outlook Conference." Each State extension service sends two or more delegates to this meeting. In 1962 a Department employee called attention to the absence of Negro extension workers from the conferences. In 1963 Texas and North Carolina extension services sent Negro staff members to the conference and the Department sent invitations to ten Negro colleges. Tuskegee Institute responded by sending a faculty member who was not connected with extension. In 1964 only Maryland sent a Negro extension worker as a delegate. Negro colleges were again asked to send faculty members, and four did so.[41] Thus, Negro participation at the conference again was arranged for outside of the usual channels.

Professional Associations.—The professional associations of extension workers—the National Association of County Agricultural Agents (NACAA) and the National Home Demonstration Agents Association—are important instruments of professional development. The annual meetings of these organizations are designed as training centers and agents are given official study leave to attend conventions. Membership in the National Association of County Agricultural Agents, for example, is acquired through membership in the State association. In a number of Southern States membership in the State professional association has not been open to Negro extension workers. Negro county agents and home demonstration workers have formed their own State professional organizations. In recent years Negro county agents have sought without success to be admitted to State associations and to attend

[41] *Letter from FES to Commission on Civil Rights,* Sept. 24, 1964.

conventions of the National Association.[42] Officials of the Federal Extension Service have consistently attended the white segregated meetings and have worked with committees on which only the white association was represented. However, the agency's most recent Administrator has evinced concern at the exclusion of Negroes from professional gatherings.

In September 1964, the Board of Directors of the NACAA instructed the Presidents of State associations to extend to all active male extension agents an invitation to attend the National Convention at New Orleans. However, this did not occur in most Southern States. The Commission was able to establish only that the Texas extension service sent such a notice to Negro agents. The only Negro in attendance at the New Orleans meeting was a Negro agent from Texas who is the national president of the Negro professional association.[43] Federal officials were in attendance at the meetings and the meeting was addressed by a Federal official who dealt in part with the impact of the Civil Rights Act upon the Cooperative Extension Service.[44]

SERVICE TO NEGROES

Planning the Extension Program

The Commission found that the isolation of the Negro farmer and rural resident began with the extension planning process. While the involvement of local people in the preparation of the county annual plan of work is regarded as a vital part of Extension philosophy,[45] Negroes are involved in the planning process only

[42] Information is based on correspondence between officials of white and Negro county agents' associations. Copies are retained in Commission files.

[43] *Letters from FES to Commission on Civil Rights,* Sept. 28, 1964 and Oct. 27, 1964.

[44] Address by Dr. Nyle C. Brady, Director of Science and Education, USDA, at annual meeting of National Association of County Agricultural Agents, Oct. 8, 1964, New Orleans, La.

[45] A USDA Extension publication states, "the people to whom a program is directed must be involved in planning it, and programs gain by the development of procedures that let as many people as possible share in plans." *A Guide to Extension Programs for the Future: The Scope and Responsibilities of the Cooperative Extension Service, 1959,* pp. 47–48.

in those counties with Negro extension workers, where separate white and Negro advisory committees make separate plans. In counties without Negro extension personnel, however, Negroes do not share in drawing up these plans which outline the programs and goals for the county and assign to the extension staff their responsibilities for the coming year. In such counties no plan of work with Negroes is made.

In counties where Negro extension workers are assigned, the fact of segregated planning was succinctly stated by one white county agent in Alabama: "We make our plans; they [Negroes] make their plans." He advised that an all-white extension council formulated the white plans and that the Negro agent did not participate in this process. An all-Negro extension council formulated the plans for the Negro population of the county. The white county agent did not have a copy of the Negro plan of work and stated that he never saw the Negro plan. Conversely, the Negro agent had never seen a copy of the white plan and was unfamiliar with the plan's goals. The same segregated pattern was found in other States.[46]

Poor white farmers have the same agricultural problems as poor Negro farmers, just as the needs of a progressive Negro farmer for advice and information do not differ from those of a successful white farmer. Further, the Department of Agriculture itself recognizes that the economic development of a county is dependent upon a comprehensive rather than a fragmented approach to its problems: "Organized local committees, consisting of representatives from all interested groups, motivated by a desire for improvement . . . can attain an improved economy in the rural community." [47]

---

[46] This was documented in Georgia, Louisiana, Mississippi, North Carolina, South Carolina, and Virginia. In South Carolina, although white and Negro extension staff plans are combined at the county level, this consolidation is for purposes of submission to the State extension office only and is not a substantive change in the segregated system.

[47] USDA, *Rural Areas Development Handbook*, Agriculture Handbok No. 245 (June 1963), p. 1.

Assignment of Responsibility for Work With Negroes

Commission staff interviews, supported by statistical evidence, established that the Negro rural population was almost exclusively served by Negro workers and that in counties without Negro extension personnel service to Negroes was minimal.

At the State level Negro extension workers in the segregated State office were found to be responsible for work with Negro county agents, and through them for work with Negro farmers. In Louisiana this function was outlined in the State Plan of Work submitted to the Federal Extension Service in these words: "Located at the Southern University extension office are four State extension workers who perform the roles of assisting Negro parish personnel with Extension programming." [48]

Counties With Negro Personnel.—State extension officials uniformly agreed that Negroes at the county level were served by Negro agents if Negro agents were assigned there. Commission staff interviews with county agents, both white and Negro, confirmed this practice. As one white county agent in Alabama put it: "The Negro agent's responsibilities are the same as mine, only for Negroes." Another white county agent stated that he worked infrequently with Negroes, visiting Negro farms not more than 15–20 times a year but generally sending any requests from Negroes to the Negro agent. In Georgia, a white home demonstration agent referred Negro callers to the Negro associate home demonstration agent since "they are her constituency." Another white home demonstration agent met with the County Council of Negro Home Demonstration Clubs five months prior to the Commission on Civil Rights staff interview but since that time she had rendered them no other service. In Louisiana a white agent stated that the white staff would not organize Negro home demonstration clubs. Such requests were referred to Negro workers. Describing this referral to a Negro worker, a Louisiana State extension official said this was "as it should be." Although a white agent had helped

[48] USDA FES Files, Plan of Work, Louisiana Agricultural Extension Service, Project VII, July 1964–June 1965, p. 22. Similar structure was also documented in Alabama, Georgia, Mississippi, and Virginia.

white farmers expand into poultry, both at their request and upon his own initiative, he had never done so for Negroes. Similar patterns prevailed in Mississippi, South Carolina, and Virginia.[49]

Counties Without Negro Personnel.—In the absence of Negro personnel some agricultural services were provided to Negroes by white personnel. However, one Louisiana State extension official said, "I would not want to leave the impression that their responsibility has been discharged equally." Especially when the two extension programs of 4-H and home demonstration clubs were discussed, most extension officials agreed that it was unusual to find a program for Negroes in a county without Negro workers.

In Mississippi a State official said that when he was a county worker, both races came to his office and he helped them both. A county agent in that State asserted that he spent much of his time working with Negroes. Nevertheless, this same county agent who said he worked with Negro farmers did not know if Negro children went to 4-H camp, indicating that this was not part of his responsibility. In the same county the white home demonstration worker did not work with Negro women. In Virginia a State extension official agreed that service by whites to Negroes in 4-H and home demonstration work would be exceptional.

Louisiana State officials said white staff in the absence of Negro workers would organize Negro 4-H and home demonstration clubs though not "as much as we would like." But a list of Negro home demonstration clubs furnished to the Commission by the State Extension staff showed that no Negro home demonstration club was reported in any parish without either male or female Negro personnel. With the exception of one parish with a small Negro population, the same was true for Negro 4-H clubs. In

---

[49] In Virginia a State extension official observed that the races "tend to go to the office of the agent of their own race." In Mississippi one county agent characterized the Negro agent as "the coordinator of Negro programs." Another agent stated that "Negro staff are responsible for work with colored." In one South Carolina county the Negro assistant county agent worked only with Negroes but the white staff provided livestock advice for Negroes. In another county the agent estimated that a substantial number of visits were made by white staff to Negro farms, a fact disputed by a local FHA worker who stated that the white agent does not normally work with Negroes except when Negroes come to his office for soil testing.

761-685 O—65——4

North Carolina no Negro 4–H clubs were reported in any county without Negro agents.

Assignment of Personnel To Work With Negroes[50]

State officials explained that the placement of Negro personnel was determined by the availability of Federal, State, and county funds, the willingness of the county to have a Negro worker, and the size of the Negro rural population. The State would not place a Negro in a county if there were strong sentiment against it.[51] This local option to reject personnel assigned to work with Negroes was noted in the 1939 study of county agents.[52] Because counties may refuse to accept Negro agents and have done so despite State efforts to the contrary, there was no close correlation between rural Negro population and Negro extension employment.

In every Southern State the number of extension workers assigned to work with Negroes was grossly disproportionate to the numbers of Negro families they were expected to serve when compared with the white assignments.

Even if the "separate-but-equal" doctrine were acceptable as a standard, any claim of equality of service to Negroes would require that the ratio of extension workers assigned to the Negro population be the same as that for whites. Such was not found to be the case. Commission staff interviews in the counties visited revealed either inadequate numbers of Negro workers or the total absence of Negroes assigned to work in counties with high Negro populations.

In an effort to secure a broader perspective, 125 counties which had the highest number of Negro farm operators were chosen in each of five States and the pattern of extension staffing studied.[53]

---

[50] Commission investigation found that extension personnel assigned to work with Negroes were consistently Negroes themselves. In the discussion below such workers are termed "Negro Agents," a term used in the county offices. In February 1963 there were about 500 counties in the South with such workers.

[51] This was documented in Georgia, South Carolina, and Virginia.

[52] Baker, *op. cit.*, p. 199.

[53] Alabama, Georgia, Louisiana, Mississippi, and South Carolina. For detailed list of counties and statistics, see app. D.

There were white agents and home demonstration workers in all 125 counties.

Caseloads in Counties With Negro Agents.—In those selected counties where some Negro staff were assigned, a comparison with population statistics established that, with some exceptions, the Negro workers had a potential caseload at least twice that of the white staff. In youth work the potential caseload of Negro agents often was three or more times higher than that of whites.[54]

Table 1.—*Number of farm operators and rural boys aged 10–19 years, for each male extension worker, by race, in selected counties[1] with Negro staff*

State:	*Farm operators*		*Rural boys*	
	White	*Negro*	*White*	*Negro*
Alabama	312	796	323	1,203
Georgia	391	373	403	872
Louisiana	344	634	375	1,209
Mississippi	310	954	315	1,356
South Carolina	499	945	948	1,967

Number of rural households and rural girls aged 10–19 years, for each female extension worker, by race, in selected counties[1] with Negro staff

State:	*Rural households*		*Rural girls*	
	White	*Negro*	*White*	*Negro*
Alabama	1,435	2,287	427	1,346
Georgia	1,612	1,310	520	789
Louisiana	1,942	2,099	892	1,202
Mississippi	1,211	2,603	394	1,504
South Carolina	3,210	2,985	1,163	2,018

[1] The 25 counties in each State with the largest number of Negro farm operators were selected. For detailed discussion of counties studied and method of selection, see app. D.

Caseloads in Counties Without Negro Agents.—Of the 125 selected counties, 42 were without Negro agricultural agents. These 42 counties contained 27,000 Negro farmers, or 26 percent of all Negro farmers in the 125 counties. In Georgia, Louisiana, and Mississippi, more than one-third of the Negro operators and Negro rural youth in the studied counties were in counties with-

[54] Georgia's relatively low caseload for Negro workers must be viewed in the light of the extensive absence of Negro staff from the counties with high concentrations of Negroes. This is particularly true of youth work. South Carolina's showing of equal figures for adult home demonstration work results from the very high white caseload rather than an improvement in service to Negroes.

out Negro agents. Assignments of Negro home demonstration workers left similar gaps in the population of the studied counties. Fifty-six thousand Negro rural families were in the 38 counties which had no Negro home demonstration agent. In Georgia, for example, nearly 75 percent of the Negro girls of 4–H Club age in the counties studied lived in counties without Negro home demonstration workers. The families of these girls, representing 55 percent of all rural Negro households in these counties, were, of course, similarly without service. In Louisiana 43 percent of rural Negro households in the counties studied were without Negro agents.

Staffing in counties without Negro personnel was examined to determine whether the number of white personnel was sufficient to provide service at a reasonable level to both the white and Negro population. The addition of Negro youth and rural households to the caseload of white extension staff would have resulted in a caseload double that carried by white staff in other counties except in South Carolina where caseloads for whites were already very high. Substantial but less severe increases in white caseloads would result if Negro farm operators were included in the caseload of white agents.[55]

The Quality of Service to Negroes

Experience in other educational fields has shown that under segregation Negroes do not receive equal treatment.[56] Extension education proved to be no exception. To acquire an understanding of the services rendered Negro rural families, a more intensive review of the service provided was necessary along with some attempt to measure the effectiveness of these services when compared to the services received by white families. The Federal Extension Service had not, within recent years, attempted to review the quality and quantity of the racially segregated services offered

---

[55] See app. D. table III.

[56] *Brown* v. *Board of Education,* 347 U.S. 483 (1954). See also U.S. Commission on Civil Rights, *Equal Protection of the Laws in Public Higher Education* (Washington: U.S. Government Printing Office, 1960).

Negroes in the Southern States. However, FES officials have re-emphasized the need for evaluating extension services and have indicated that they were "seeking more effective ways to do the job." [57] In initial interviews Federal officials insisted that no records were kept on the basis of race and that it was, therefore, impossible to evaluate the agency's work with Negroes. Efforts to carry out such an evaluation were considerably hampered by the inadequacies of data collected by the FES and available to the Commission. Commission staff undertook to review such data as was available in an effort to arrive at preliminary findings. This data was then supplemented by Commission field studies. While more conclusive in some areas than others, this review identified discriminatory and unequal treatment in Extension programs.

Service to Farmers.[58]—A sampling of county plans of work and annual reports reflected the pervasive basic assumption that there are two distinct Southern agricultural economies—one white and the other Negro. Although in no way conclusive, the sampling of annual reports indicated that Negro farmers in the South were not participating in services reported for whites in the same county.

In North Carolina a white agent reported that county livestock problems had been solved but the Negro agent reported a high swine mortality rate for the same year.

In an Arkansas county, according to the annual report, soil specialists met with white farmers to solve pasture problems. The Negro agent reported that same year that Negroes received their information on the subject through lectures by local farmers. Where a special program of intensive Farm and Home Development for low-income families was carried on, the white county agent spent an average of 6 man-days with each such family, while the Negro agents spent only 3 man-days per Farm and Home Development family in the same year.

[57] *1965 Appropriations Hearings*, pt. 2, p. 367.

[58] Documentation in this section is from files of the Federal Extension Service, County Annual Reports, and from field interviews. Separate plans of work and annual reports for white and Negro county staff were filed with the FES until 1960. These were made available to the Commission for study. Some county reports for later years were secured by the FES also and reviewed.

In a Florida county, where storage of corn was a problem, the white agent's annual reports for 2 years noted that farmers had been assisted in obtaining bins through the Commodity Credit Corporation loan program. The Negro county agent reported each year that many Negro farmers were selling surplus corn due to lack of storage space.

In Georgia, a white agent's annual report emphasized that shrinking tobacco allotments had pointed to the need for a program to promote sweet potatoes, while the Negro report did not mention diversification and spoke of increasing tobacco yield. Differences in the treatment of problems related to tobacco were also revealed in reports from a North Carolina county. The white agent's goal was to increase tobacco income by $160 per acre, while the Negro agent's goal was simply to realize a profit above labor costs. In a South Carolina tobacco county the white agent, in his annual report, stated that Blue Mold damage to tobacco was slight; in the same year the Negro agent reported that farmers were unable to get enough young tobacco plants because of Blue Mold.

While evidences of unequal service to Negro farmers were difficult to identify in the field, some clear instances of a double standard came to the Commission's attention. In an Alabama county the Negro agent stated to Commission interviewers that Negroes did not attend demonstrations held on white farms and that there were beef cattle demonstrations for white farmers but none for Negroes. Negro agents in two other Alabama counties reported that the unavailability of a financial sponsor prevented the holding of a tractor maintenance clinic and a "fat calf show" for Negroes. In another Alabama county, specialists met with white farmers while the Negro agent reported that Negro farmers did not receive the services of specialists. Another Negro agent said that he had learned, through conversations with white livestock producers and newspapers, about a fertility testing program for bulls which was available to white farmers but not to Negroes.

In one Louisiana parish without a Negro agricultural agent the county agent had not included any of the Negro dairymen in a program intended to improve dairy farm management by encouraging better record keeping in dairy production. Furthermore, he had taken the initiative in suggesting diversification to poultry farming with white farmers, but had never done so for Negro farmers.

In South Carolina a white county agent reported that on assignment to the county he found white farmers reluctant to undertake dairying and he was proud of his success in overcoming their apathy and getting them into dairying operations. The Negro assistant agent stated that Negroes were not in dairying because, among other reasons, they would require special training. In this county no such training has been provided by the extension service for Negroes. The Negro agent said he was concentrating on the "family cow."

In some instances where the only extension staff responsible for Negroes in a county is the Negro home demonstration worker, Negro farmers must rely on her to perform agricultural work normally assigned to agricultural agents. One Louisiana white agent stated that he used the Negro home demonstration worker for contact with farmers, "although being a woman [she] is not trained in this particular field." In another parish the Negro home demonstration agent reported that Negro farmers were referred to her for agricultural programs by the white office which had five professional men for such work. When she attempted to organize a seed and fertilizer cooperative for Negro farmers this Negro home demonstration agent requested the assistance of the white agent. He referred her to an assistant who said he was too busy to help her. She finally requested assistance from a member of the staff of a Negro land-grant college at the opposite end of the State. The annual report for a Mississippi county with four white male agents showed that the Negro home demonstration worker performed agricultural services normally expected only of male agents. Similarly, a Negro home demonstration worker in a Tennessee county was reported as having spent many days of work with farmers on livestock, crops, marketing, soil conservation, forestry, wildlife, farm business, and mechanical equipment. The Commission staff did not find white home demonstration agents doing similar agricultural work.

The establishment of lower goals for Negro farmers is one of the most serious handicaps of the segregated extension service. Speaking to his fellow Negro agricultural workers years ago, the president of Mississippi's Negro land-grant college decried the emphasis on subsistence in Negro extension services—"Live at Home" for Negro farmers but "Plant to Prosper" for white farmers: [59]

> There is nothing wrong in differing. By all means, let us be original. But if that originality is not just as good or better than the other fellow's slogan, let's not be original. Why two anythings when one will do just as well? . . . Catch phrase programs and wishful thinking may give glamorous publicity, but they don't keep Negro farmers from losing their farms in the Tennessee Valley and other choice farming areas of the South and Nation.

Low expectations of Negro achievement were reflected or implied in statements made by both white and Negro State Extension Service officials. Commission staff were told that "corn is just not a Negro crop;" that Negroes do not follow extension service recommendations; that "we often fail to understand the irresponsibility of the Negro race;" that sheep field days are held only for whites since "Negroes don't have any interest in sheep;" that no extension assistance is needed by Negroes because "there is every indication that they have discovered a way to make a living;" that Negroes are incapable of organizing for rice farming since they have more than they can take care of; "that if you could have dairying from Monday to Friday, many Negro farmers would be dairymen; but since it is a 7-day business, Negro farmers won't work 7 days." Even an official of the Federal Extension Service stated that Negroes "have gone about as far as they can go."

---

[59] J. R. Otis, *Trends in Agriculture Since 1910,* Proceedings of Tuskegee Rural Life Conference, June 18–29, 1950 (Tuskegee Institute, 1950), pp. 46–47.

Service to Rural Households.—Home demonstration agents work directly with rural and farm women in their homes and through home demonstration clubs. Programs are designed to help the whole family by assisting the homemaker with family budgeting and meal planning, home management, child care, clothing, the family garden, and many other activities. However, the opportunities for Negroes to acquire information and assistance through the home demonstration program was also found to be severely limited. It was generally conceded that there is no organized home demonstration program for Negro women where there are no Negro extension personnel employed. White agents did not organize and rarely assisted the Negro home demonstration program.[60]

A white home demonstration agent in a Louisiana parish provided information to Negro women if they visited her office or if she visited white homes in which Negroes were employed as servants or where Negro tenants were present. While she sometimes visited white families without a request being made for her services, she had never visited Negro families without a request. In another parish the white home demonstration agent stated that she did not invite Negro women to an educational meeting because she "didn't think about sending them invitations." In Louisiana parishes where only male Negro workers were employed they were said, by a State extension official, to be responsible for Negro home demonstration work as well as their other duties.

In North Carolina counties without a Negro home demonstration worker, Negroes could organize informal clubs on their own which, while not considered in the same category as other home demonstration clubs, could receive assistance from the Extension Service.

The failure to serve Negro rural families in important areas of home demonstration work, which was freely admitted in field interviews, was identified through an analysis of annual reports in Extension Service files. In three States studied, the proportion

---

[60] This was documented in Louisiana, Mississippi, North Carolina, South Carolina, and Virginia.

of Negro rural households reached with these programs was half that of white rural families.

Table 2.—*Percent of rural households reached with Home Demonstration Programs by race 1960*

	Alabama		Georgia		Louisiana	
	White	Negro	White	Negro	White	Negro
Home management	20	9	10	3	29	15
Family economics	9	4	6	4	16	6
Clothing	44	19	29	9	55	22
Food and nutrition	47	22	42	17	69	38
Health	21	10	20	14	20	22
Family life	24	10	15	5	20	9

Source: FES, Statistical Summary, 1960, items 64 and 70, *1960 Census of Population,* PC (1) B, vol. I, table 19.

In these States there was a high proportion of counties without Negro home demonstration workers.[61] Mississippi and South Carolina, in contrast, with higher proportions of Negro home demonstration workers, reported almost equal service to Negro and white rural households.

If the need for the assistance of home demonstration workers is measured by family income, the inequality of service to Negroes is intensified, for the median income of Negro rural families with children in these States was about half that of similar white households.[62]

Service to Youth.—A further measure of the human cost of the segregated and unequal structuring of extension services can

[61] Number of counties with home demonstration agents by color of agents:

State:	*White*	*Negro*
Alabama	67	35
Georgia	139	39
Louisiana	64	20
Mississippi	82	55
South Carolina	46	33

Source: *County Agents Directory, 1961.*

[62] Income of families with own children under 18, *1960 Census of Population,* PC(1)D, table 140.

be found in the services to youth. The exclusion of Negro youth from service is well illustrated by one Louisiana county agent who had notified only white high schools of a recruitment program for students of veterinary medicine. When asked why he had not notified Negro high schools he said, "It just really didn't occur to me, actually."

Extension services to youth, however, are primarily channeled through the 4-H club program. Federal Extension officials have stated that work with Negro youth through the 4-H clubs is a very important service rendered by extension agents to the rural Negro population. According to an Extension publication:[63]

> Club work contributes to communities and community life in many ways—developing leadership among adults and youth, teaching youth skills and techniques, developing a positive attitude toward future learning, and physical community improvement resulting from activities.

Recognizing the importance of this program Negro agents often reported spending 60 percent or more of their time working with Negro youth in 4-H club work.

And yet the Commission found serious inequities in the white and Negro 4-H clubs in terms of number of clubs, number of youth enrolled, number and types of programs and activities, and number of extension agents assigned to work with 4-H clubs.

The 4-H club program operates at the county, State, and national levels. Two major national events—the National 4-H Club Annual Conference in Washington and the National 4-H Club Congress held annually in Chicago—afford recognition to youth who have been outstanding club members in their States. And yet, while these events receive considerable support and assistance from the Federal Extension Service, Negro youth from the Southern States have been excluded from participation because of discrimination and inequities in State 4-H programs and methods of selecting delegates.

---

[63] Dr. E. T. York, Jr., "What is the 4-H Story?", *Extension Service Review*, February 1962, p. 27.

Delegates to the National 4-H Club Conference held annually in Washington [64] are selected in the various States from among members nominated by county agents on the basis of 4-H achievement, citizenship, and leadership ability. In 1964 only North Carolina among the Southern States considered Negro youth for nomination as delegates to the national conference, and North Carolina alone of the Southern States sent a Negro member as a delegate. Prior to 1961 Negro 4-H club members from the Southern States had been confined to a segregated "Regional" conference held at Howard University, also in Washington. The elimination of this segregated meeting was not accompanied by any safeguards to assure that Negro youth would be included in the National 4-H Club Conference, and so their exclusion from the national scene was continued.

Negro youth have also been excluded from the National 4-H Club Congress held annually in Chicago [65] to provide recognition of 4-H club achievement in specified project areas for which national awards are set. At these conferences youth who have been chosen as State winners compete for national awards, usually $500 scholarships, sponsored by large commercial and manufacturing concerns which serve the agricultural economy. The National 4-H Service Committee which sponsors the Congress, has established a "Special Awards" program for Negro youth in 17 Southern States which provides a $50 bond for each Negro State winner in a project area but excludes the Negro youth from attending the national congress and from competing for the many $500 scholarships offered. In 1964 only North Carolina considered the achievements of Negro youth in choosing State winners, and a Negro youth from that State was a State project winner.[66] The separate

[64] Held under the auspices of the National 4-H Club Foundation, a private organization which includes the Administrator of the FES among its officers.

[65] Held under the auspices of the National 4-H Club Service Committee, "a nonprofit corporation organized by public-spirited citizens who believe in 4-H as a valuable training ground for our nation's youth. The organization utilizes private resources to assist the Cooperative Extension Service in advancing the membership, leadership and influence of the 4-H program." *Souvenir Program*, 43d National 4-H Club Congress, p. 32.

[66] *Letter from FES to Commission on Civil Rights*, Dec. 14, 1964.

awards system did not include any recognition of achievement in project areas of citizenship, home economics and public speaking for which white youth were awarded prizes.[67] Despite this continued exclusion of Negro youth the 4–H Club Congress in 1964 was addressed by the director of Science and Education for the USDA and five FES officials, including the assistant director of 4–H and Youth Development.

In Louisiana six white youth went to Philadelphia as the winners of a State sweet potato contest from which Negroes were excluded; three white youth went to Kansas City, Missouri after winning a poultry contest from which Negroes were excluded. Similarly, four whites represented Louisiana at the National Junior Vegetable Growers Association. Denied the opportunity to compete for national awards, 24 Negro youth were sent on a trip to Mexico City sponsored by friends of 4–H.[68]

Many Negro youths were barred from participation in 4–H clubs at the county level. State extension officials in Mississippi, North Carolina, and South Carolina agreed that where there were no Negro agents in a county, there was no 4–H program for Negro children. In Georgia, Louisiana, and Virginia the officials admitted there were few exceptions to this rule. Statistical analysis confirmed this. Of Louisiana's 63 parishes where white 4–H programs were carried on, 26 provided no Negro 4–H program whatsoever. Twenty-eight percent (26,000) of all rural Negro

---

[67] "Regulations All 1964 Special State 4–H Award Programs" published by the National 4–H Service Committee. Some examples of unequal prizes listed for whites and Negroes in the *Handbook of Louisiana Awards, 1964:*

"a. 'Bread'—the white State winner goes to Chicago to compete for one of six $500 scholarships and the Negro State winner is eligible for a $25 bond.

"b. 'Tractor-driving'—white youth in each district compete for three sets of hand tools. Negroes have a medal for four parishes only and one statewide $50 bond. Whites have a chance at a national scholarship award. Negroes do not.

"c. Electric—white boy and girl winners in each parish have choice of several small appliances and in each district compete for a $100 selection of equipment, while the State winner goes to Chicago to compete for six $500 scholarships. Negro winners get one medal for each parish and one State winner is eligible for a $50 bond."

[68] Louisiana Agricultural Extension Service, *Annual Narrative Report for 1963, Project No. 6, 4–H Club*, pp. 35 and 95.

youth of 4–H club age lived in those parishes.[69] Similarly, in North Carolina all of the 100 counties had white 4–H programs; but nearly half offered no 4–H club program for Negroes, although 25,000 rural Negro boys and girls of 4–H club age lived in those counties, constituting 15 percent of all such youth in the State.[70]

Where there is a 4–H program for Negroes, as with other segments of the Extension Service, it is organized, administered, and staffed entirely by Negroes. As has been shown, these Negro extension workers have youth caseloads three and four times as high as their white associates. They must rely upon the Negro community for leadership and assistance in their programs. The result of this segregation was that even when Negroes were provided with services which made 4–H club membership possible, the quality of program carried on was seriously deficient when compared with that conducted for white youth.

Thus, in Alabama in 1960 (the last year for which figures were reported to FES) while each white 4–H club member was reported as receiving training in a number of subjects, there were 24,000 Negro members reported who were not receiving training in any 4–H club subject. This was epitomized in the case of health and nursing where only 717 of 17,600 Negro girls in 4–H were enrolled, although more than half the white girls in 4–H clubs took such training. Similarly, 1 out of 32 Negro 4–H members were trained in thrift, while 1 out of 4 white members took such training. Only 3 percent of Negro youth, but 90 percent of white youth, received citizenship training.[71]

The training and projects for Negro youth were severely restricted in Louisiana's 4–H program. Negro youth had less than half as many projects per person as their white counterparts. The failure to prepare Negro youth for a nonfarm future was particu-

---

[69] Louisiana Agricultural Extension Service, *Annual Narrative Report, 1963,* Negro Enrollment by Parishes and Projects.

[70] Memorandum from State Extension Official for 4–H Club Work, North Carolina, undated (copy retained in Commission files). In both Louisiana and North Carolina the Negro population was computed from *1960 Census of Population,* vol. I, table 29.

[71] FES, Annual Reports, Statistical Summary, 1960.

larly noticeable in a selected group of projects designed to help improve the social and economic opportunities of the youth where Negro participation was only half that of whites.[72] On the local level this meant that in one parish only 1 of 50 Negro youths were enrolled in a tractor project while 1 out of 6 white youths were so engaged.

In one Georgia county, although membership in clubs was about equal for whites and Negroes, Negro enrollment in important projects was a fraction of that for whites.[73]

Table 3.—*Lowndes County, Ga., 4–H enrollment in selected projects*

	Average for 3 years	
	White	*Negro*
Membership	900	900
Projects:		
Health and nursing	700	40
Child care	120	28
Junior leadership	88	27
Farm and home safety	850	110
Citizenship	800	37
Personality improvement	420	122

Similar differences in services rendered Negro and white youths were found in South Carolina and in Alabama.[74]

[72] Projects included: Automotive, electricity, child care, citizenship, home management, junior leadership, money management, health, and others. Louisiana Agricultural Extension Service, *Annual Narrative Report for 1963,* Project No. 6, 4–H Club, pp. 9–10. An example of the limitations experienced by Negro 4–H club programs was found in Louisiana where a white county agent reported the placement of 13 heifers with 4–H club members by a dairy calf chain in 1958. The Negro agent reported a lack of funds to purchase calves for Negro 4–H members.

[73] USDA FES Files, Lowndes County Annual Reports, 1958–60.

[74] In a South Carolina county there were specialized clubs in electricity for whites but not for Negroes. In another county whites participated in a greater range of activities than Negroes and visited industrial plants while Negroes did not since they could not secure transportation. In one Alabama county white 4–H members and leaders were taken on a tour of Birmingham steel plants but Negro 4–H members had no such trip. Another Alabama county reported other field trips for white 4–H club members and a complete absence of such trips for Negro 4–H youth.

Summary

Largely in response to local pressures, and as a result of the statutory requirement of dual control by Federal and State governments, a segregated system of service to Negroes has been built into the Extension Services in the South. Segregation has permeated extension activities in three crucial areas—planning, personnel, and services. Furthermore, it has occurred at all three levels of government—Federal, State, and county.

Although Negroes form a substantial portion of the population on the basis of which Southern States receive their allocation of Federal extension funds, Negroes have not shared equitably in the services provided by such funds. At the Federal level funds, supportive services, and professional assistance have been channeled into the segregated system without adequate safeguards to assure equality of distribution, while Federal personnel have participated in and encouraged activities from which Negroes were barred.

At the State level separate staffs have been maintained under the extension director, with white specialists in technical subject matter (agronomy, entomology, horticulture) and Negro "specialists" who all too often have been specialists only by virtue of the fact that they served Negroes. Programming, training, and services have generally been kept separate and unequal both in quantity and quality.

At the county level the effects of the double standard have been clearly manifested in the isolation of Negro staff in inferior offices with inadequate supportive services in those counties where Negroes were employed. In counties where there were no Negro workers, Negro farmers have been excluded from institutionalized activities and generally disregarded by white staff.

The weight of evidence available to the Commission indicates that the Federal Extension Service, by acquiescing in the determination by others of what Negroes should and should not receive in many counties of the South, has often permitted Negro farmers and rural residents to be partially deprived or wholly cut off from those benefits which the agency was originally established to provide.

III. THREE DIRECT FEDERAL PROGRAMS OF ASSISTANCE TO FARMERS

Three agencies of the Department of Agriculture which administer direct Federal programs on a county level serving farmers and rural residents are the Farmers Home Administration (FHA), the Soil Conservation Service (SCS), and the Agricultural Stabilization and Conservation Service (ASCS). The first is a loan program, the second provides professional services for landowners and associations, and the third administers the acreage allotment and price support programs and makes grants for conservation practices. In each program local control of the decision-making process is of considerable importance. For FHA this is achieved through county committees appointed by the Federal Government, for SCS through elected boards of supervisors, and for ASCS through elected committees. These programs are considered together because they are similar both in their administrative structure and in the kinds of civil rights problems their operations involve.

FARMERS HOME ADMINISTRATION

Credit, capital and equipment were the crying need of Southern agriculture as seen by a commentator in 1889: [1]

> Tobacco and cotton flourish here as nowhere else and rice, sugar and naval stores add millions annually to its wealth;

[1] Blair, Lewis H. (C. Vann Woodward, ed.), *A Southern Prophecy:* The Prosperity of the South Dependent upon the Elevation of the Negro (1899) (Boston: Little, Brown, 1964), pp. 30–31.

761-685 O—65——5

> but although this production has been going on uninterruptedly for more than twenty years her people are not rich, but on the contrary are very poor. They are not only burdened with debt up to their full capacity for borrowing, but much, if not the greatest part, of their crops is made by loans, beginning with the time of planting. Their home are not only unsupplied with many of their most essential comforts, but their plantations are ill supplied with stock and implements. . . . The want of accumulated capital is extreme, and for at least six months of the year, money, instead of being a reality, is rather a thing of memory and of hope . . . with the greater part of the people.

More than 40 years later expanded farm credit was part of the New Deal program, first in relief measures and finally as part of an overall attack upon the farm tenancy problem.[2] It was Senator John Bankhead of Alabama who designed and fought for the Bankhead-Jones Farm Tenant Act of 1937.[3] At that time Senator Bankhead inserted in the Congressional Record statistical summaries showing the high incidence of farm tenancy in the South and the high proportion of Negroes who were tenants. In support of the legislation he said, "More than half of the farm tenants, regardless of their intellectual standards, and regardless of all other considerations, have a longing for homes of their own for themselves and for their families."[4] Senator Tom Connally of Texas insisted that the tenants needed "not charity . . . but the opportunity to work out their own salvation on the soil . . ."[5] and said that one of the purposes of the bill was "to cause the Government . . . to take steps . . . so that each one may have a place which he can own and hold, not under feudalistic title . . . and from which he can look the

---

[2] Seed, crop, and feed loans had been available from the Federal Government since 1916. (Federal Farm Loan Act, 39 Stat. 360). The New Deal program added farm ownership loans and other assistance. *Century of Service, supra*, pp. 214–215.

[3] 50 Stat. 522 (1937).

[4] 81 Cong. Rec., 6667 (1937).

[5] *Id.*, 6686.

world in the face and not be disturbed by waves of industrial and economic unrest." [6]

The program of low-cost credit and supervised farm management seemed ideally suited to raise the Negro tenant from his depressed condition. Yet, during a quarter century of operation the program has not made substantial inroads upon the problem of tenancy for Negroes. While the proportion of full tenancy among white farmers in the South fell from 46 to 17 percent from 1935 to 1959, more than half the Negro farmers (52 percent) remained tenants in 1959, a reduction from 77 percent. Among white farm operators in the South, only 10 percent remained in sharecropping, the lowest economic level among farmers, while among Negroes 40 percent remained sharecroppers.[7] Whites in all tenure classes have increased the size of their farms while for Negroes the increase has been minuscule, and a rapidly widening disparity in the size of farms between whites and Negroes has occurred during this quarter century.[8] The number of farm operators has dropped sharply in the South, but the number of Negro farmers dropped more rapidly than whites between 1935 and 1959. White farm operators declined by one half but the number of Negro farm operators fell by 75 percent in the same period. Thus, while Negroes constituted a quarter of the Southern farm operators in 1935, by 1959 they were only 16 percent.

The acquisition of additional land during this period was the key to remaining in agriculture on an economically sound basis. In 1959 Southern white farmers were operating 3 million acres more than in 1935, but Negro acreage had dropped by 22 million.

[6] *Id.*, 6678–6679.

[7] *1959 Agriculture Census*, vol. II, ch. X, table 5.

[8] Land in farms by color and tenure of operator for the South, 1935–59:

	Average acreage 1935			*Average acreage 1959*		
Tenure	*White*	*Negro*	*Negro difference*	*White*	*Negro*	*Negro difference*
Full owners	125	57	—70	162	62	—100
Part owners	246	56	—190	469	83	—386
Tenants	97	40	—57	200	35	—165
Cash tenants (1940 data)	158	50	—108	422	53	—369

Source: *1959 Agriculture Census*, vol. II, ch. X, table 7.

About 19 million acres were withdrawn from farming altogether, and white farmers absorbed the additional 3 million lost by Negro farmers.[9] Small farmers, white and Negro, continue to disappear from the scene with each agricultural census. However, during the quarter century since the farm credit program of the New Deal undertook to help tenants achieve ownership and to help small farmers enlarge their operations, the position of the Negro farmer relative to white Southern farmers has steadily worsened. Although all small farmers have been subjected to severe economic strain, Negro farmers have been more sharply reduced in number, lost more acreage, and remained concentrated in the least advantageous tenure groups and crops.

While in other years appropriations for the farm ownership program may not have been equal to the task, since 1961 funds have been increased and the program invigorated.[10]

The purpose of this study is to determine whether the programs of the Farmers Home Administration, designed to promote enlarged and more efficient family farms, are currently providing the remaining Negro farmers with equal service.

Administrative Structure and Program

The Farmers Home Administration, unlike the Cooperative Extension Service, is a direct Federal program administered from Washington through State and county offices all staffed by Federal employees. At the county level eligibility for assistance is determined by a committee of three local residents appointed by the State director.[11] The State directors also have committees of State residents, federally appointed, who advise on policy and procedures.

---

[9] *Ibid.*

[10] "Dramatic increases" from 1960 to 1962 in farm ownership loans, particularly in Arkansas and Mississippi, were noted by members of the House Appropriations Committee. These were explained by the Administrator of FHA in terms of increased funds available and as largely for improvement in the land base of inadequate units. *1964 Appropriations Hearings*, pt. 4, p. 2167.

[11] 7 U.S.C. 1982 and 6 C.F.R. 301.3(c).

The program is primarily one of loans to farmers combined with technical assistance to "help family farmers acquire the resources needed for successful operations that will bring these families up the economic ladder." [12] To accomplish these objectives, loans, accompanied by technical assistance, are made to individual farmers for the acquisition or enlargement of farms, the acquisition of livestock or equipment, the purchase of seed and fertilizer or other annual operating costs, the refinancing of chattel debts, the improvement of farm buildings, and the construction or improvement of farm homes. To be eligible for such loans the applicant must establish to the satisfaction of the three-man county committee that he is of good character, capable of repaying the loan, and cannot secure credit on reasonable terms in the commercial market.[13]

In addition to its program of economic improvement for farmers, in recent years the FHA has given increasing emphasis to strengthening rural communities and furnishing leadership for rural programs to combat poverty. The agency has proposed to "ease the burden of poverty" through subsistence loans and housing grants for families "who are handicapped by age, color, education, physical and mental defects . . . and thereby unable to escape the poverty level." [14]

FHA's programs are carried out through 1,500 offices located in most rural counties throughout the nation, staffed by county supervisors, who may have one or more assistants. State offices provide supervision, coordination, and staff and management services, including in-service training.

At the end of fiscal year 1963 the FHA was servicing accounts of 230,000 borrowers with outstanding indebtedness of $2.1 billion. It had at that time about 5,000 full-time employees, and there were 5,900 State and county committeemen considered part-time employees.[15]

---

[12] Purpose Statement, *1965 Appropriations Hearings,* pt. 4, p. 295.

[13] USDA, FHA, *Farmers Home Administration in Brief* (PA 547, February 1964).

[14] Purpose Statement, *supra,* note 12.

[15] *1964 Appropriations Hearings,* pt. 4, p. 2155 and *1965 Appropriations Hearings,* pt. 4, p. 288.

Negroes in the FHA

In its national and State offices and its 1,500 county offices, FHA has about 40 Negroes employed as professionals.[16] Of approximately 3,600 State and county committeemen in the South holding office under Federal appointment in 1961, none were Negroes. As of October 1964, 9 Negroes had been appointed as State Committeemen in the 16 Southern States, and 116 Negroes had been appointed to county committees, 100 serving only as alternates.[17]

FHA's use of Negroes in its administrative structure has conformed to the patterns of a segregated society. As a professional worker and as an alternate committeeman the Negro in FHA in the South plays a separate and subordinate role, frequently as an appendage to the general administrative structure.

The Use of Negroes as Committeemen.—In counties where Negroes constitute a majority of low-income farmers, the absence of Negroes from the committee structure has seriously handicapped the development of full participation by Negroes in the new and growing agricultural economy. In 1962 when there was increased awareness of the need to include Negroes on county committees, the FHA responded by appointing Negroes to a newly created category of *alternate*. The statute establishing the committee system had always provided for alternates, but this position had previously been used primarily where one committee served several counties. In such cases, the alternates reviewed only applications filed from their own counties. Negro alternate committee members proved for the most part to be superfluous and inoperative.[18]

---

[16] USDA, FHA document prepared for Commission use in August 1964 entitled *Negro Personnel in Program Positions* (undated) (copy retained in Commission files).

[17] USDA, FHA document prepared for Commission use entitled *Negro County Committeemen* (copy retained in Commission files). Negroes are now serving as regular committeemen in Arkansas, Indiana, North Carolina, and Oklahoma. Negroes have been appointed as State committeemen in Alabama, Arkansas, Florida, Georgia, Louisiana, Mississippi, North Carolina, South Carolina, and Texas.

[18] 7 U.S.C.A. 1982 creates the position of alternate committeeman and provides that the number of days and rate of pay shall be determined by the Secretary. White alternate committeemen have not been paid or required to attend meetings when the full committee was present. For the Negro alternates a new position was created and they were paid for all meetings attended whether or not a regular committee member was absent. This payment in no way mitigates the fact that they are relegated to a subordinate role.

Field investigations indicated that there was considerable confusion about the role of the Negro alternate committeeman. In one Alabama county the Negro was asked his opinion on all applications, even when three members were present, and signed certificates of eligibility when a member was absent. In one South Carolina County he participated only when a member was absent, and in another did not sign certificates of eligibility even in the absence of a member because two members constituted a quorum.

The appointment of Negroes to the county committees did not cause any adverse community reaction according to both State directors and white supervisors in the counties visited. One exception was reported in a State where some white county committeemen had threatened to resign if Negroes were appointed. However, none did so when the appointments were made. There was some indication that the communities would have accepted the appointment of Negroes as full committeemen as easily as they accepted their appointment as alternates. It was not clear that all communities realized that the Negroes were appointed as less than full committeemen. Based on their experiences with the Negro alternates, some State directors expected to have Negroes as full committeemen in the near future.

The Use of Negro Professionals.—In the 1930's and 1940's, the Farm Security Administration, predecessor of the Farmers Home Administration, had a substantial number of Negro employees in the South, including a Negro professional who headed an all-Negro office with an all-Negro committee.[19] Some of the 22 Negro assistant county supervisors in the South started with the agency at that time. Gradually, the all-Negro offices were eliminated and by 1964, with the exception of a single office in Florida, the remaining Negro professional county workers were in offices with white employees.

Despite this move into the white offices, however, the Negro employees of FHA in the South administratively were a separate group of Federal employees. This was true of the one Negro

[19] USDA File AD 130–02—Negroes, Reports to Will Alexander, 1942.

employed in the national office of FHA, the Negroes with statewide responsibilities employed in 10 Southern States, and the 22 Negroes employed as assistant county supervisors in the Southern States.[20] This small group of Negro employees formed a separate and unique administrative structure limited to serving Negro borrowers.

The Commission found that there was a Negro FHA employee stationed in Washington whose title was "Farm Management Representative (Program Officer)." He traveled extensively in the South and at the request of State directors called upon difficult or delinquent Negro borrowers, particularly in the areas where there was no Negro county staff. Occasionally, he worked out a farm plan for a successful Negro borrower.

In the 10 States where there were Negroes employed at the State level, they had a title held only by Negroes—"Program Staff Assistant."[21] In Louisiana, Oklahoma, and Virginia, these were the only Negroes employed by FHA. In 4 of the 10 States (Louisiana, Mississippi, Oklahoma, Tennessee) the Negroes thus employed were not located in the State office where the other State-level FHA employees were housed. In Louisiana the State worker was found at a land-grant college where he was without a telephone and not listed either in the local phone book or in the Departmental Directory. The other three were located in county offices at some distance from the State office. For instance, the program staff assistant in Mississippi was promoted to this position in 1963 but in 1964 was still in the same county office where he had worked as an assistant county supervisor. The Negro statewide employee in Virginia had been located at the Negro land-grant college[22] for eight years until July 1964 when he was moved to the State office.

Negroes with statewide responsibility served in part as roving assistant county supervisors for the counties without Negro staff.

---

[20] The four Negroes employed in county offices outside the South, including two in California as heads of county offices, are presumed to work across color lines but have not been studied. USDA, *Negro Personnel in Program Positions, supra.*

[21] Letter from Acting Administrator, FHA, Nov. 19, 1964.

[22] This office was not listed in the USDA, *Directory of Organization and Field Activities,* 1962.

In some States a considerable portion of the program staff assistant's time was spent on Negro delinquent borrowers. These workers were also responsible for working with Negro county extension agents and with Negro organizations to bring an understanding of FHA programs to them.

Lines of authority for these Negro workers were unclear. In one State the Negro worker felt he could initiate contact with Negro farmers anywhere without consultation. In another State, the State director spoke of the program staff assistant as "more or less a free agent," making his own itinerary and submitting recommendations to the county supervisor or area supervisor. Community hostility toward Negro State workers sometimes limited the activities of Negro workers in a county. In one State, the Negro State worker did not attend regional staff meetings in one section of his State because, as he said, of the "thinking" of the area's white residents—despite the fact that a great many Negro borrowers lived in that part of the State. On the other hand, in another State where county personnel threatened to close the office if the Negro State worker were sent there, the State director was successful in insisting that they respect the position of the Negro worker. Local resistance in another State was not permitted to block the hiring of a Negro assistant supervisor after the Washington office insisted upon its right to place a Negro there.

The 22 Negroes employed at the county level all work as assistant county supervisors.[23] Twelve have been hired since 1962. These assistants served only Negro borrowers and were limited in training and promotional opportunities. Opportunities for promotion from assistant to county supervisor were nonexistent for Negro workers in the South. This was true even in offices where a majority of the borrowers were Negroes. Nine of the Negro assistant county supervisors had 15 to 25 years of service at the county level in such positions. Where promotion above assistant supervisor had taken place it had been to a State position, but not to that of county supervisor.

---

[23] FHA document, *Negro Personnel in Program Positions, supra.*

There was some evidence that Negro assistant supervisors were also restricted in training opportunities. Distinct differences were noted in the training given two employees hired about the same time—one white and one Negro—in the same State. In that State the Negro trainee worked only with Negro applicants, and his experience tended to be limited to the smaller, less diversified, predominantly low-income farmers in his county. The white trainee had the broader experience of working during his training period with both white and Negro applicants. The white staff person had numerous contacts with the county committee, both in the training office and after assignment to his home office. The Negro trainee had not, when interviewed, attended a meeting of the county committee in his training office or in his home office. The white trainee had been personally introduced by his county supervisor to the white extension agent, soil conservationist, and ASCS office manager. The Negro trainee had not been introduced to any other agricultural personnel and had sought out the Negro county agent on his own.

Though Commission field investigators were told of a few instances where Negro staff had demonstrated their ability to work with whites, these successful experiences had never led to nondiscriminatory assignment of duties. One Negro assistant supervisor reported that in 1947 he had filled out a new form of loan application for a white applicant who looked him up and exchanged greetings on many subsequent occasions. The Negro employee, however, never again served that white applicant or any others. Two Negro State FHA workers reported they had occasionally been given the names of delinquent white borrowers (by mistake they believed) and had handled the assignments successfully.

The Commission found that, unlike the pattern of extension work, Negro clientele of the FHA were served by both white and Negro FHA staff. With one exception, Negro borrowers were served in the same office as white borrowers.

Service to Negroes

From the beginning the task of FHA was to break the vicious cycle of farm tenancy and debt, to make the tenant farmer an owner and help him "to look the world in the face." To achieve these purposes with Negroes in the rural South the FHA would be required to provide the Negro farmer with a combination of loans and technical assistance which would equip him to master new, diverse, and larger farming operations and to improve his grasp of financial management and planning. FHA has been providing this kind of help to poor small white farmers in the South, but it has not given comparable service to Negro farmers similarly situated either in terms of the size of loans, the purposes for which the loans are to be used, or the technical assistance necessary to fully achieve the purposes of such loans.

In 16 Southern States FHA has increased the number of all loans by 25 percent since 1960. The percentage increase was about the same for Negro and white borrowers. In 1964 in these States 4.7 percent of white operators and 5.7 percent of Negro operators received FHA loans.[24]

The number of loans made to Negroes, however, is only one important measure of service provided. To adequately evaluate FHA's programs required more detailed information than was readily available. At the request of the Commission, detailed data covering the period July 1963 through May 1964 were obtained on borrowers in 13 counties, selected from the basic list of 71 counties with heavy Negro concentration in agriculture.[25] The

[24] USDA, FHA, *Letter of November 2, 1964*. Actual figures given were:

	1960		*1964*	
	White	*Negro*	*White*	*Negro*
Loans made	40,728	8,462	54,336	10,985
Loans per 1,000 farm operators	29.6	31.1	47.0	56.6
Percent change—1964 over 1960 in loans per 1,000 farmers			58.8	82.0

[25] Counties selected by FHA were—Alabama: Greene and Wilcox; Arkansas: Lee and Phillips; Mississippi: Holmes and Madison; North Carolina: Columbus and Duplin; South Carolina: Georgetown, Orangeburg, and Williamsburg; Tennessee: Fayette and Haywood. Data are contained in tables retained in Commission files. The full report of statistical analysis of the figures has been prepared as an appendix to this report and may be secured by writing to the Commission.

data were subjected to statistical analysis. The findings, which were discussed with officials of FHA, are summarized in the following section.

From these figures certain generalizations can be made. FHA was, indeed, making a considerable number of loans to Negroes in these counties. Actually the number of loans to Negroes in these counties was somewhat more favorable than for the South as a whole, with FHA loans reaching 5.6 percent of Negro farmers and 3.5 percent of white farmers. In these counties 1,733 farmers borrowed $6.3 million from FHA. Thirty-three percent of the borrowers were white and received 66 percent of the funds while Negroes, who constituted 67 percent of the borrowers, received 34 percent of the funds.[26] Negroes constituted 55 percent of all farm operators in these counties.

These disparities, however, are not meaningful in view of the wide disparity in net worth [27] between white and Negro farmers in the study group. There may be other variables which affect the size and type of loans and the quality of technical assistance provided to borrowers by FHA, but within the limits of data provided, an analysis of difference in services by net worth, geographic area and race was deemed significant. Since the size of a loan would logically bear some relationship to net worth, it was necessary to break down the loan data to arrive at a comparison of loans to white and Negro farmers in the same economic class as defined by net worth. The resulting distribution showed that the great majority of the Negro borrowers were in the two lowest classes; in the top three classes whites outnumbered Negroes, and in class IV they were about equal.

---

[26] Size of loan varied from $100 to $30,000 with the average loan to whites at $7,000 and to Negroes $2,000.

[27] Average net worth, according to FHA, is as good an index of economic class as is available. The average net worth of all white borrowers was $10,000 and for nonwhites was $4,000. The average for white and Negro net worth in each class does not vary widely.

Number of borrowers by race and economic class (net worth—figures rounded)

	Negro	*White*
Class I (over $20,000)	10	90
Class II ($15–20,000)	20	80
Class III ($10–15,000)	50	110
Class IV ($6–10,000)	130	110
Class V ($3–6,000)	270	90
Class VI (less than $3,000)	680	80
Total	1, 160	560

The loans to whites and Negroes in the same economic class were then compared for size of loan and purpose or use to which the loan was put.

Size of Loans.—For both whites and Negroes the largest loans went to the farmers with the highest net worth. But there the

FIGURE 1. AVERAGE LOAN SIZE BY RACE AND ECONOMIC CLASS

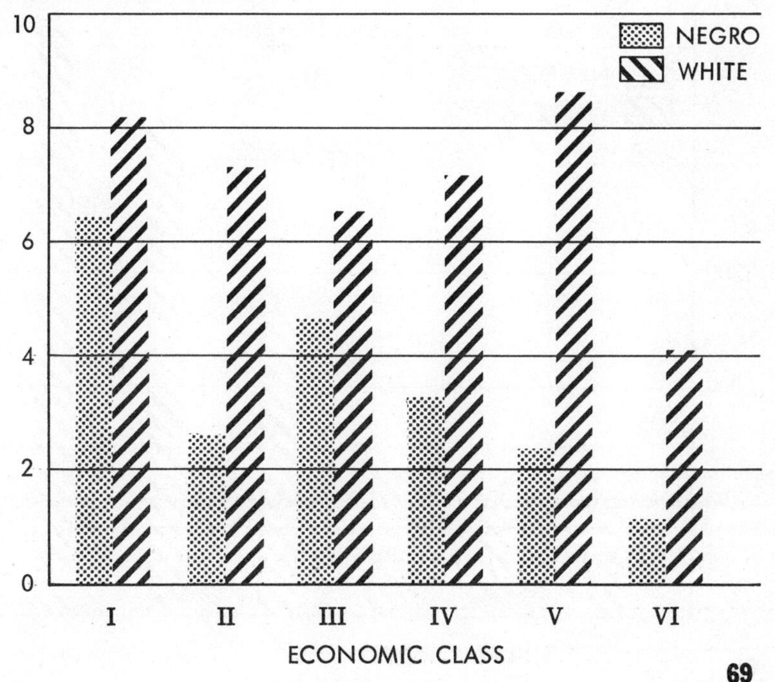

similarity between the races ended. In each economic class, average loan size to whites was substantially greater than for Negroes. Furthermore, as can be seen in figure 1, the average size of loans in classes III through V, where the majority of white borrowers were found, increased steadily as net worth decreased. Thus, progressively larger amounts were made available to poorer white farmers. For Negroes, however, the trend was reversed and the average size of loan in these classes dropped sharply as the poorer farmers were reached. The result of these contrasting trends was that the disparity between whites and Negroes in average size of loan increased as the borrowers got poorer, until in classes V and VI the average size of white loans was four times that received by Negro borrowers.

This reversal of trends according to the race of borrowers is even more apparent in figure 2, showing the number of dollars loaned

FIGURE 2. AVERAGE LOAN SIZE PER $1000 OF NET WORTH BY RACE AND ECONOMIC CLASS

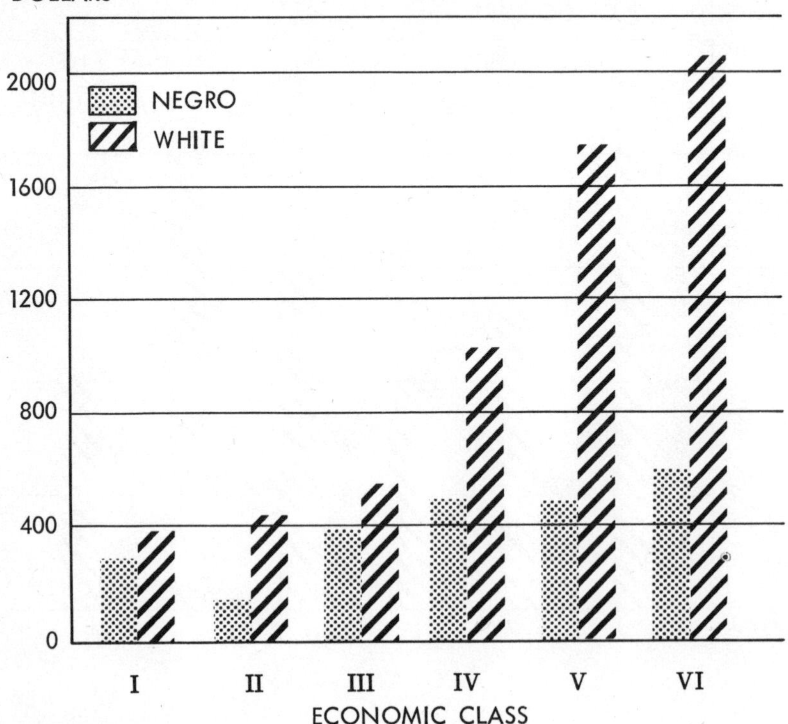

per $1,000 of net worth. Here the figures for white borrowers showed a steady progression upward of loan-to-worth ratio from the richest to the poorest, until at class VI white borrowers were receiving loans proportionately five times as large as those received by richer white borrowers. For Negroes no such upward trend in benefits provided poor borrowers was shown, the increases being slight. And poor white borrowers received both absolutely and proportionately higher loans than poor Negro borrowers, who constituted a majority of the Negro borrowers.

Purpose of Loans.—All the funds considered were loans for purposes which fell into four categories: [28]

1. Operating loans for specified uses, as follows:
   Family living expenses;
   Farm operating expenses;
   Livestock purchase;
   Farm equipment purchase;
   Real estate improvement;
   Refinancing of chattel debts.
2. Farm ownership loans—to acquire or enlarge farms.
3. Rural housing loans for both farm and nonfarm homes.
4. Emergency loans—to carry on or restore normal operations.

[28] For Operating, Farm Ownership, and Rural Housing Loans initial and subsequent loans were combined, as no significant differences in such loans was discerned in the counties studied.

A borrower is not left to decide for himself what kind of loan he will request and receive. The FHA staff plays a vital role in helping him decide the uses to which FHA funds will be put. An interview with one State director established that FHA has played a substantial role in encouraging diversified farming. When a farmer comes in to apply for a loan, the FHA county supervisor often takes the initiative, and recommends the acquisition of additional land, enlarged allotments, off-farm employment, soil conservation assistance, and the use of extension specialists or other educational resources to improve the economic position of the farmer.

While the Commission did not attempt to evaluate the relative importance of different kinds of loans, significant differences were found in the type of FHA loans received by white and Negro borrowers. In the following charts [29] loans for living expenses, farm operating expenses, and emergencies are listed in that order. These are characterized as used for current expenses. They are followed by loans for farm improvement (which includes loans for purchases of livestock and equipment as well as loans for real estate improvement), refinancing of chattel debts, farm ownership and rural housing—all of which are characterized as used for capital investments.

The kinds of FHA loans available to white and Negro borrowers have been summarized in figure 3 by grouping uses into two categories. On the left-hand side of the chart are grouped loans for current expenses—living expenses, farm operating expenses, and emergencies. On the right-hand side are grouped those loans used for capital expenditures—housing, farm ownership, real estate improvement, livestock and equipment purchases, and refinancing chattel debts. It is quite clear from this chart that the trends in use of funds are moving in almost exactly opposite directions for Negro and white borrowers. Poor whites receive FHA assistance to acquire or expand their farms, to stock and equip them, and

[29] In these summaries and charts, loans in Arkansas have been excluded because they reflected a drought in 1963 which greatly increased both the size and number of emergency loans, thus distorting the figures for all counties.

to improve their housing or their financial position. This is rarely ever the case for Negroes. For each successively lower economic class of Negro borrowers FHA assistance goes more heavily to living expenses and annual operating costs.

FIGURE 3. EXPENDITURES OF FHA FOR CAPITAL EXPENSES AND CURRENT EXPENSES BY CLASS AND RACE

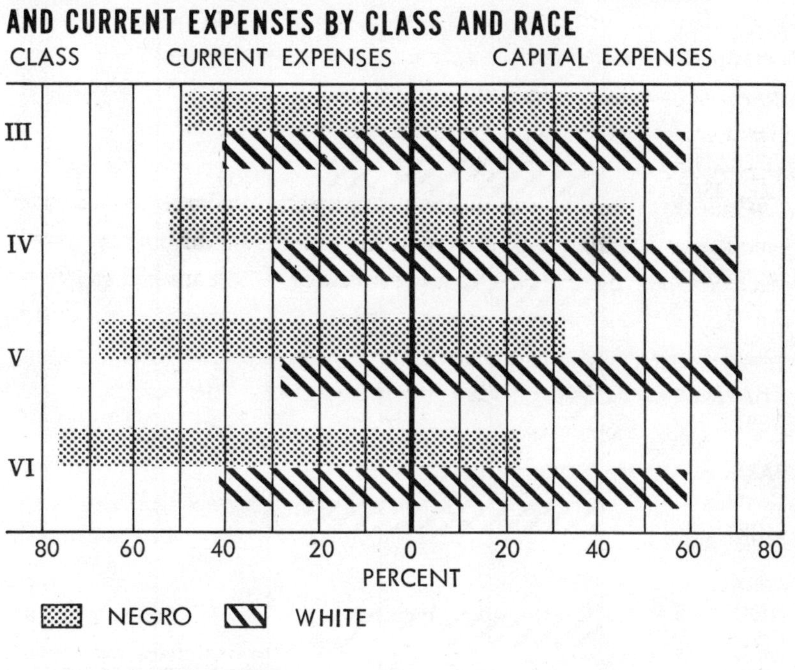

For all economic classes of borrowers combined certain clear disparities in use can be noted (fig. 4). The fact that Negro borrowers received half the amount loaned to white borrowers in proportion to their numbers increases the disparities. Furthermore, 63 percent of all funds for Negroes went for living expenses, annual operating expenses, and emergencies, but only 34 percent of the much larger amounts received by whites went to these purposes. Almost 50 percent of white funds went for acquisition of land or housing, but only 25 percent of Negro funds were so used.

761-685 O—65——6

FIGURE 4. USE OF FUNDS LOANED TO ALL CLASSES OF FARMERS BY RACE (PERCENT DISTRIBUTION)

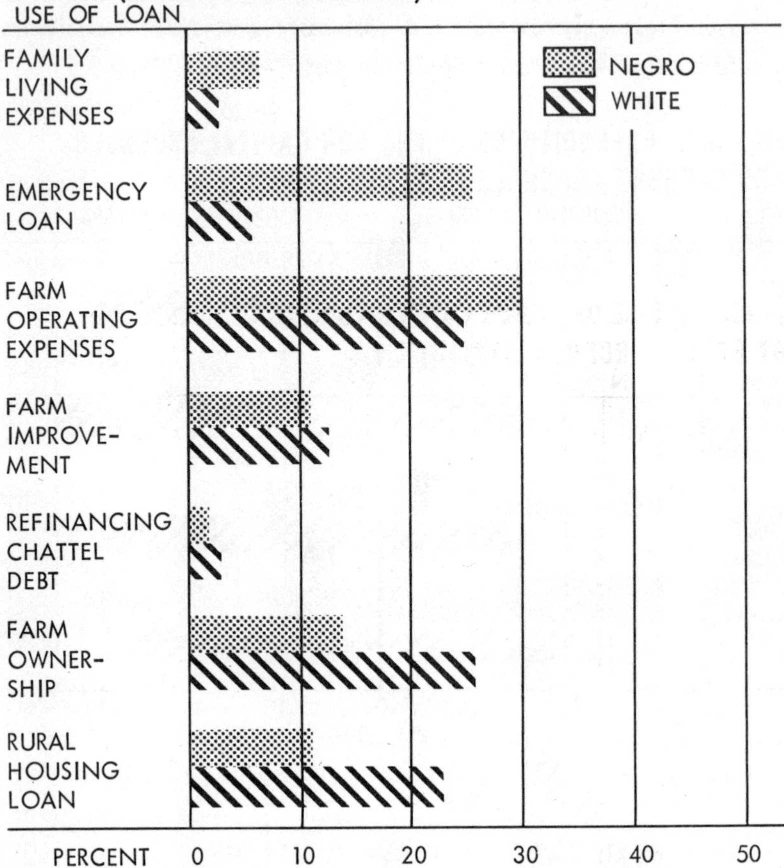

Of all the funds loaned by FHA in the studied counties 25 percent went to white borrowers for farm ownership or housing and only 8 percent went to Negroes for this purpose. For the acquisition of farms alone, 17 percent of total funds went to whites and 4 percent to Negroes.

Again, however, these figures reflect to some extent the concentration of Negroes in the lowest economic class. For instance, one-third of all funds for Negroes went to one class—the poorest borrowers—for living, operating, and emergency expenses. It is important, therefore, to compare the uses for which loans were made to whites and Negroes in the same economic class. No comparisons were made for classes I and II because in some counties no Negro borrowers appeared at this level. Therefore, class III is the highest level of economic class for which comparisons are made. At that level the significant disparity is in the percentage of funds received as emergency loans—24 percent for Negroes and only 9 percent for whites. Whites and Negroes received approximately equal percentages of funds for farm ownership, and Negroes received a slightly larger percentage for farm improvement (fig. 5).

FIGURE 5. USE OF FUNDS LOANED TO CLASS III FARMERS BY RACE (PERCENT DISTRIBUTION)

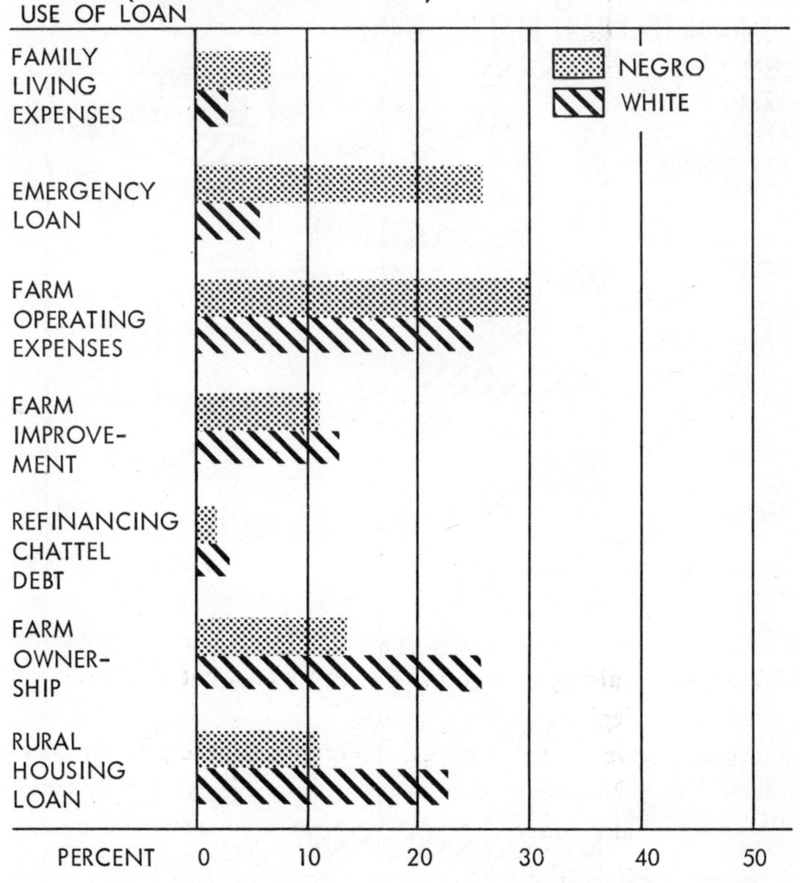

The same criteria applied to farmers in class IV begin to demonstrate the trend which becomes more evident at still lower economic levels. Emergency loans are one-fourth of Negro funds but only 4 percent of white funds. On the other hand, rural housing loans are 32 percent of white funds but only 12 percent of Negro funds. The proportions received by each race for farm ownership loans is about equal (fig. 6). When stated in dollar terms, however, this apparent equality disappears because of the larger average size of loans received by whites. Thus, class IV white received $130,000 to acquire or enlarge farms, but similarly situated Negroes received only $80,000. There are slightly more Negroes than whites in this class.

FIGURE 6. USE OF FUNDS LOANED TO CLASS IV FARMERS BY RACE (PERCENT DISTRIBUTION)

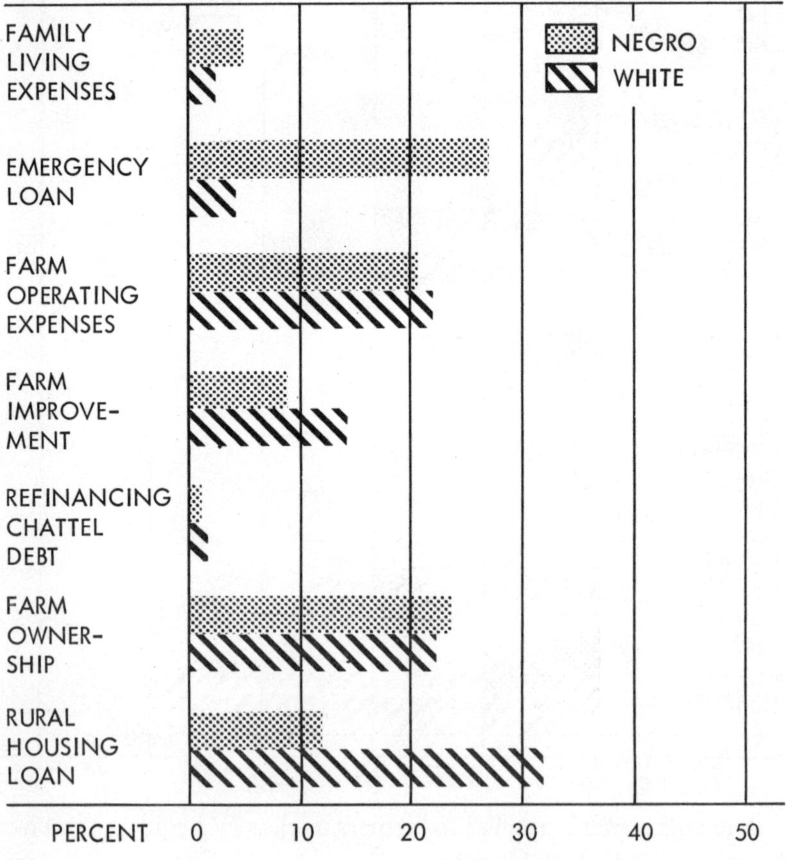

In class V poor white borrowers received 25 percent of their funds for living, operating, and emergency uses while Negroes received 68 percent for these purposes. White borrowers in class V received 65 percent of their assistance from FHA to acquire farms, farm land, or housing while for their Negro counterparts such assistance constituted only 20 percent (fig. 7). In this class, where Negroes outnumber whites 3 to 1, whites received farm ownership loans totaling $81,000 while the Negro figure was $30,000.

FIGURE 7. USE OF FUNDS LOANED TO CLASS V FARMERS BY RACE (PERCENT DISTRIBUTION)

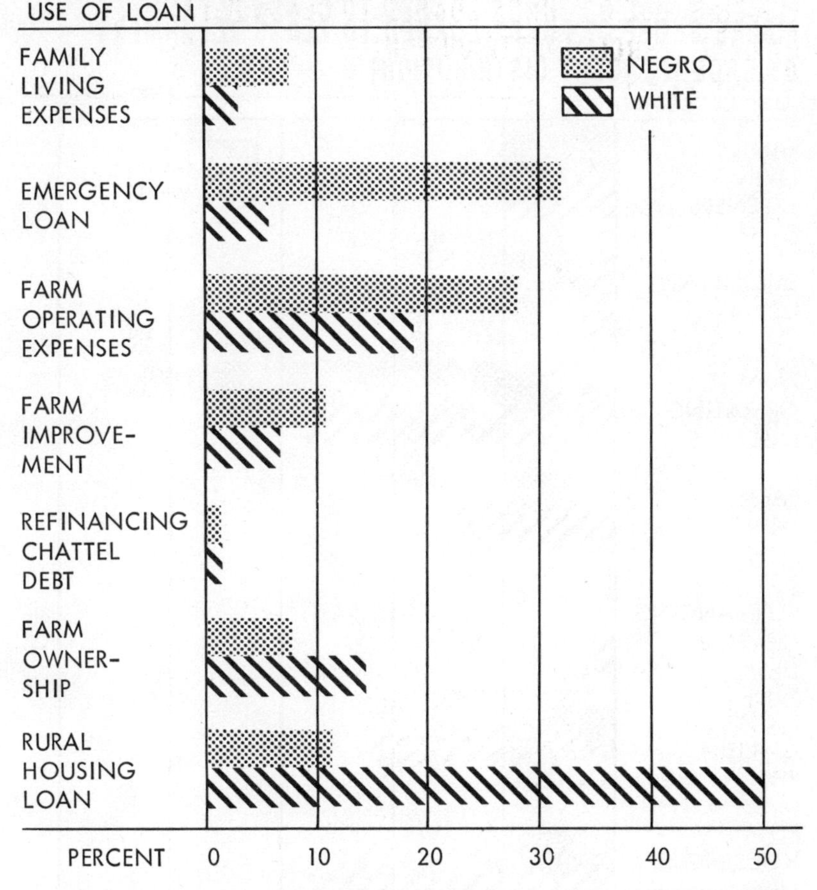

It is at the lowest economic level, where average white loans are four times as large as those received by Negroes, that the disparities are most extreme. Here 77 percent of FHA assistance to Negroes took the form of living expenses, operating expenses, and emergencies. Poor white borrowers, however, received only 41 percent of their FHA assistance in this category. The poorest white borrowers received 28 percent of their assistance for housing and an additional 11 percent for acquisition or enlargement of farms compared to 10 and 3 percent, respectively, for Negro borrowers (fig. 8). The dollar totals for farm ownership loans in class VI were almost the same for whites and Negroes—about $18,000 for each group—but there are eight times as many Negroes as whites in this lowest class.

FIGURE 8. USE OF FUNDS LOANED TO CLASS VI FARMERS BY RACE (PERCENT DISTRIBUTION)

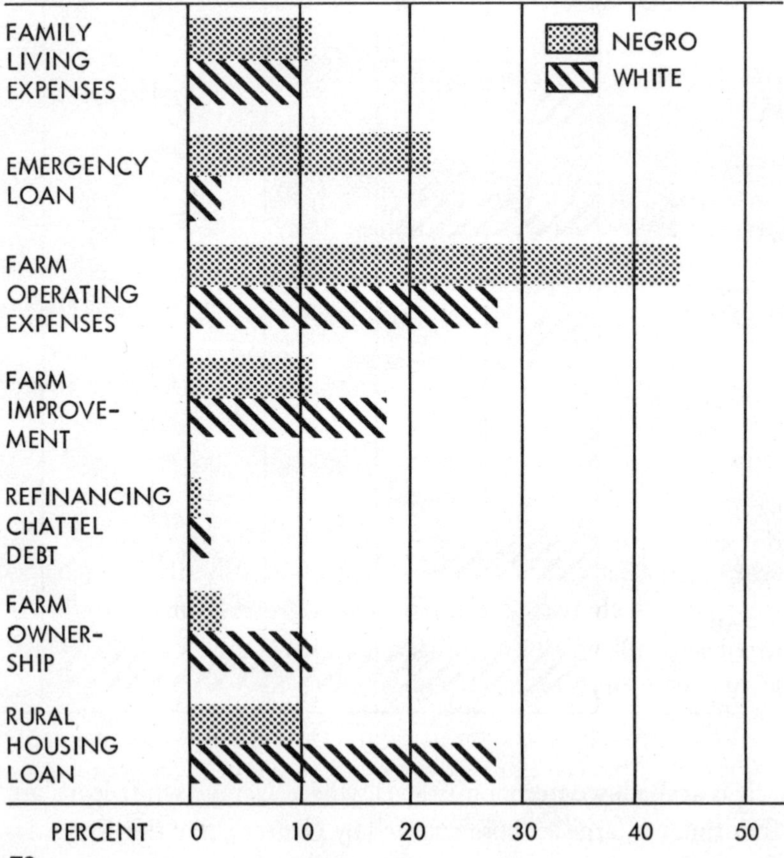

Technical Assistance to Borrowers.—Undergirding the whole loan program of FHA is the concept that credit must be combined with technical assistance on farm and home management to enable borrowers so to modify their practices that their farms will become economically viable. Secretary Freeman has described this education process as follows: [30]

> These borrowers received technical supervision as well as credit. The Department helps them work out and maintain both yearly and long-term farm and home development plans. At least once each year, FHA supervisors help them review their year's operation, with special emphasis on production, financial management, marketing, household spending, and other farm and home planning.

FHA calls the provision of such technical assistance "supervision" and provides for two types of supervision—intensive and limited. Intensive supervision involves strong emphasis on farm and home management as well as financial management. On a national average intensive supervision includes four and a half farm visits a year, scheduled to coincide with the application of a new practice or some other critical point in the farm development plan. Furthermore, the year-end review of progress under the plan, to which the Secretary referred, is generally made only for loans under intensive supervision. Limited supervision, on the other hand, provides for fewer farm visits and does not carry as much emphasis upon money management and farm practices.[31] The crucial role of intensive supervision in diversification and economic improvement can be seen from the fact that FHA instructions to county offices state that intensive supervision will ordinarily be given to "families which will depend primarily upon farming for their livelihood and will be making major adjustments and improvements in their farm and home operations . . ." In contrast,

[30] USDA, *Report of the Secretary of Agriculture,* 1963, p. 16.

[31] FHA Instructions for limited supervision require "at least one" farm visit per year and emphasize personal contacts "when the loan is delinquent." USDA, FHA Instruction 430.1, *Supervision-General.*

limited supervision is to be provided for those families which either are not primarily dependent upon their farms for their livelihood or are not making major changes.

The income of the borrower and the size of the loan do not determine the type of supervision. As an FHA official stated, the determining factor is understood to be the need of the farmer for assistance in making changes. The agency has indicated to Congress that "with low-income farm borrowers, it is particularly important to provide good technical supervision and assistance coupled with needed credit, if the borrower is to become successfully established." [32]

Clearly, the distinction between intensive and limited supervision is of considerable importance to the small, poorly educated Negro farmer if he is is to have any hope of adjusting his farming operation to meet modern needs, both in terms of diversification and production methods.

FHA publishes statistics by State showing the percentages of borrowers receiving intensive and limited supervision. At the request of the Commission FHA submitted additional tables showing this data for Negroes in the Southern States.[33] These tables revealed that in the 11 States where loans to Negro farmers are concentrated, substantially higher proportions of Negro borrowers than whites were receiving only limited supervision.

For those borrowers operating "adequate farms," the proportion receiving intensive supervision was about equal for whites and Negroes (74 and 68 percent, respectively). However, only 42 percent of Negro borrowers as compared to 62 percent of white borrowers operated "adequate farms." Negro borrowers were found predominantly among those with "inadequate farms," and it was among this class of borrowers that the amount of supervision given was drastically unequal for Negroes. While over 34 percent of white borrowers with inadequate farms had intensive super-

---

[32] Purpose Statement, *1965 Appropriations Hearings*, pt. 4, p. 295.

[33] The following section is based on published and specially prepared data submitted to the Commission by the FHA as follows: *Weekly Loan Report*, Fiscal Year 1963, Cumulative as of June 30, 1963, and "Total Number of Initial Loans Obligated by Type of and Number and Percentage to Negro Applicants" for the same period.

vision, only 14 percent of the Negro borrowers in this group received intensive supervision. This pattern was similar to that found in the analysis of size of loans and use of loans, where the poor Negro borrowers were consistently given less money for less productive purposes than white borrowers similarly situated.

When both classes of borrowers—those with adequate and those with inadequate farms—were grouped the discrepancy was striking. Only 41 percent of white borrowers received limited supervision, but 63 percent of Negro borrowers were so served.

While there were some differences among the States, significantly differential treatment between Negro and white borrowers in both classes was found everywhere except in Mississippi (where poor white borrowers were numerous).

When these findings were discussed with FHA officials, they explained the relative lack of supervision of Negro borrowers by the fact that Negro farmers are concentrated in production of row crops. It was said that where a farmer is growing a traditional crop, he does not need supervision as much as a farmer whose crops are diversified. Here again, the current condition of the Negro farmer is permitted to limit his access to the education and assistance he needs to change his disadvantaged status. The problem is compounded by the concentration of FHA assistance to Negroes in the form of emergency loans which, according to an FHA official, ordinarily receive no supervision.

Attitudes of Field Personnel.—In its examination of FHA programs the Commission found that by all relevant criteria—size of loans, purpose of loans, technical assistance and supervision—Negro farmers were receiving less in the way of benefits than were white farmers of comparable economic status. This failure is all the more puzzling in view of the fact that FHA's central function is to raise the economic level and increase the opportunities of low-income farm families.

One possible explanation for the statistical picture is the attitude found among some FHA staff in the field that Negro farmers could not do much better than they were doing. Thus, some county supervisors, rather than making greater efforts to improve the farm and money management practices of Negro borrowers, were clearly content to give only minimal attention and service to Negroes, feeling that nothing more was warranted. When asked why Negroes had not diversified out of cash crops into livestock and other income-producing activities in which white farmers in the same area were engaged, some county FHA officials indicated that they did not believe Negroes could succeed in a diversified modern agriculture.[34]

Such expressions of self-fulfilling prophecy by a number of the officials interviewed explain to some degree the size of loans and quality of supervision given to Negro borrowers.

Summary

The FHA, like other agricultural agencies, has tended to divorce the Negro from its regular concerns, designing for him limited objectives and constricted roles. Thus, the special category of full-time, paid alternate committeemen as an artificial appendage to a full county committee came into being. The Negro employee has been confined by training, professional status, and promotional opportunities to a special all-Negro world, where he serves only other Negroes. The FHA provides for limited services to largely marginal Negro borrowers.

---

[34] Some statements of FHA county supervisors:

(In counties where whites are diversifying to livestock and Negroes remain in cotton): "Negroes don't lean as much toward livestock."

"As a general rule, the colored race and livestock don't mix; they starve a cow to death and think a pig has to be two years old before they sell him."

"Negroes are good row crop producers but don't seem to take to livestock other than swine."

(In a county where whites are switching to vegetable farming):

"We have preached that Negroes should balance their farm plan . . . but cotton is the only crop Negroes can do anything with. Negro farmers can't see this far ahead."

(In other counties):

"About all FHA can do for the Negroes is lend them enough to make a living or keep them off welfare."

"Specialists are not needed to help plan for Negro borrowers because they are only getting operating loans anyway."

SOIL CONSERVATION SERVICE

Federal employees directly serve farmers out of county-level offices of the Soil Conservation Service (SCS). Established in 1935,[35] the Soil Conservation Service works with soil conservation districts by providing technical assistance to district cooperators, watershed groups and agencies for land use adjustment, and treatment to conserve soil and water and reduce damages resulting from mismanagement and floods. Ninety-two percent of the country's agricultural land has been organized into soil conservation districts by local landowners and operators under State enabling acts. Each district is governed by a local board of supervisors. In all Southern States Federal funds constitute 88 percent of all expenditures in soil conservation district programs, exclusive of private funds invested in conservation improvements on individual farms.[36]

Soil Conservationists act as technical advisors in carrying out work planned by soil conservation district boards of supervisors. The most common pattern in the South is for boards of supervisors of soil conservation districts to be composed of not less than five persons, two appointed by the State conservation agency and the others elected under State law.[37] SCS officials were unable to identify any soil conservation district or State board in the South on which Negroes served. They were unfamiliar with the methods of elections and unable to state whether Negroes had ever been nominated for such office or whether Negroes participated in elections. When requested by State conservation boards, SCS personnel make recommendations of persons for appointment to the boards of supervisors.

---

[35] 49 Stat. 163 (1935), 16 U.S.C. 590 a–f.

[36] For a listing of Federal funds for soil conservation in Southern States, see app. E.

[37] Alabama—Code 1940, Title II § 662; Arkansas—Vol. II, Title 9 § 9–907; Georgia—5 Ga. Code Ann. 5–2002; Louisiana—LSA R.S. 3:1207; Mississippi—MCA § 4943; North Carolina—3c G.S.N.C. 139–7; South Carolina—Code 63–121; Tennessee—TCA 43–1516; Texas—Vernon's Civ. St. Art. 165a–4, Sec. 6; Virginia—4 Va. Code Ann. 21–27.

Negroes in the SCS

Few Negroes are employed by the Soil Conservation Service. In 16 States of the South, among 6,100 total employees SCS reported 40 Negro workers as of July 1964, about half at the professional level on active duty.[38] One professional is a State office employee and 16 are assigned to work units (name given to SCS offices in conservation districts). Six of the 16 were housed in segregated, separate offices apart from the white staff serving the same soil conservation district. Two of the segregated units were at Negro colleges. At the time the Commission commenced its study, the Negro soil conservationists in three work units were housed with the Negro extension agents of the counties in segregated offices. Two such offices have been desegregated since that time. SCS stationed one Negro soil conservationist attached to a work unit in its area office while the white staff was housed in the segregated county building.

Two segregated offices of the Service were visited by the Commission—one in Virginia and the other in Louisiana. In neither case did the Negro conservationist work with whites. In both cases the Negro conservationist was serving "all the Negroes" in several conservation districts, while white conservationists in the same district served only one district or county. As with the extension service, requests for information or assistance from Negroes in a district were referred to the Negro office. In both cases field sheets of soil survey maps were kept in the white office. In both cases there was little coordination between the Negro conservationists and the white conservationists in the districts in which both worked. Thus, the Negro conservationist, like the Negro extension agent, was handicapped in his efforts to serve Negro farmers.

One of the segregated offices visited was headed by a Negro with the title and grade of work unit conservationist and was composed

---

[38] The statements in this paragraph are drawn from memoranda from SCS: *Report on Southern States—Professional Negro Employees;* and *SCS Personnel EOD Dates,* 8/12/64 (copies retained in Commission files). Two were on military leave. See also *1965 Appropriations Hearings,* pt. 2, p. 439.

entirely of Negroes. Yet, only the white work unit conservationists attended meetings of the boards of supervisors of the districts the Negro unit served. In the other segregated office, the white work unit conservationist informed the Commission staff that when he could not attend a board meeting he sent a white non-professional in his place. The Negro conservationist and his Negro technician had never attended a meeting of the board of supervisors of the districts served.

Thus, not only were the Negro farmers unrepresented on the soil conservation boards but the Negro professionals who served them did not attend meetings of the board.

As with the FHA and extension service in the South, promotional opportunities on the county level were severely restricted for Negro conservationists, except in the one instance of an all-Negro unit previously noted.

The assignment of Negro professional workers in SCS did not appear to be related to high concentrations of Negro landowners, since, of the 71 counties with such concentrations, only 6 had the services of Negro soil conservationists in July 1964.[39] In South Carolina, where there was only one Negro professional, he was assigned to Aiken County which ranked 14th in number of Negro farm owners and operators. There were indications that some Negro professional workers were placed in districts where the benefits of conservation programs to the community, such as watershed or flood control, could not be accomplished without the participation of Negroes. Thus three Arkansas counties served by a Negro conservationist had watershed activities, and an SCS official explained the presence of a Negro conservationist by saying, "When you need them [Negroes] cooperating on a watershed you can't wait a few years to see if they will come in. You have to have someone go out and work with them." In Tennessee the Negro conservationist was in an area which emphasized watershed

[39] USDA, SCS, *Work Unit Estimates of Assistance to Negro Cooperators.* One other Negro conservationist in Texas was in a county of large Negro concentration.

work, and in North Carolina the one county with a Negro conservationist is marshy and required extensive drainage to make it habitable.

Service to Negroes

As with FHA, the objectives of the SCS include helping low-income families improve their economic position through sound conservation treatment of their land. Noting that low-income farmers are usually most in need of conservation help, SCS indicated that it "helps such people to develop income-producing facilities on their land, to realize higher net farm income from new sources, and to move ahead with the jobs they can do for themselves."[40] The objectives of the soil conservation program require that work be done with small as well as large plots of land.

Despite their general commitment to these ideals of conservation, the SCS, like other Agriculture Department agencies, proved to be giving service to Negro farmers not equal to that provided whites. This was apparent in the statistics of service to Negroes prepared by soil conservation work units in the 67 counties in which Negro land ownership was highest.[41]

Service to individual owners by an SCS work unit commences with a farm plan of recommended conservation practices. In the 67 counties for which data was submitted, where the largest numbers of Negro farm owners are concentrated, 66 counties reported that soil conservationists had prepared one plan for every four white farm owners. Only one county reported less—an average of one plan for every five white farm owners. But for Negroes only a third of the counties reported one plan for every four Negro farmers. In 41 counties the participation of Negroes in the program was much lower, as will be seen in the following table:

---

[40] *1964 Appropriations Hearings*, pt. 2, p. 941.

[41] USDA, SCS, *Work Unit Estimates of Assistance to Negro Cooperators*. For detailed analysis see apps. F and G. Because of the presence of large numbers of Indians, Robeson County, North Carolina and McCurtain, Muskogee and Okfuskee Counties in Oklahoma were omitted from the Commission's analysis.

Number of soil conservation service plans per farm owner, by race, selected counties

	Number of counties reporting	
	White	*Negro*
One plan for each 4 farmers or better	66	26
One plan for each 5 to 8 farmers	1	24
One plan for each 8 to 12 farmers	0	5
Fewer than one plan for each 12 farmers	0	12

In the last category participation by Negroes is as low as one plan to every 61 Negro owners in Duplin, North Carolina, one to 31 in Orangeburg, South Carolina, and one to 27 in Shelby, Tennessee.

By another measure of service, number of acres planned for Negroes and whites, the same disparities are shown. A substantially smaller proportion of Negro-owned land is covered by SCS plans. In many counties the differences in proportion between white- and Negro-owned acreage were pronounced, as seen in the following table:

Proportion of acreage in SCS plans, by race of owner, selected counties

Percent of land under SCS plan:	Number of counties reporting	
	White	*Negro*
Less than 25	1	35
25 to 74	32	27
75 to 89	13	3
90 to 100	21	2

In 9 counties among the 67 studied almost equal proportions of Negro and white acreage or over 50 percent of Negro acreage was reported as having an SCS plan.[42] In five of these counties Negro soil conservationists were serving Negro farm owners.[43] For three of the remaining counties other explanations seemed apparent. In

---

[42] Crittenden and Lee, Arkansas; Taliaferro, Georgia; Holmes, Madison and Marshall, Mississippi; Haywood and Madison, Tennessee; and Dinwiddie, Virginia.

[43] Crittenden and Lee share the services of a Negro conservationist. Madison, Tennessee has one; there is also a Negro conservationist in the State office, who assists in Haywood County, and Dinwiddie County, Virginia, has a Negro conservationist.

two, the relative equality reflected not a high degree of service to Negroes but the fact that service to whites was below 50 percent;[44] in another, the high proportions of land in timber rather than farms distorted all figures so as to make interpretation difficult.[45] In the remaining county 77 percent of Negro-owned land and 54 percent of white-owned land had benefited from SCS planning. Apparently the white conservationist in this district had found a way of working with Negro owners.[46]

The positive results achieved in a few counties suggest that a large area of unserved Negro-owned land in the other counties studied could profit from the services of soil conservationists. For where a Negro employee has been assigned this task specifically, or where a white conservationist has undertaken to perform the work, both the Negro farmers and the over-all conservation program have gained.

Discrepancies in service were found even between white and Negro farmers with the same size of farm. An additional yardstick was applied to the reported service in six counties of Alabama, where it was possible to ascertain the number of white and Negro farmers owning farms in the acreage range for which application of conservation practices was reported.[47] The conservation practices reported were those for which cost-sharing by the Federal Government was available, thus making it a particularly attractive program.[48] Yet in these 6 counties, where Negroes owned 48 to 60 percent of the farms of a fixed size, they installed only 17 to 18 percent of the farm ponds and where they owned 62 to 69 percent of the acreage, they engaged in only 33 to 43 percent of the pasture improvement; where they owned 68 percent of the acreage they applied only 49 percent of the terracing.

SCS officials in Washington cooperated in accumulating and analyzing the statistical data contained in the report. What is

[44] Holmes and Marshall Counties, Mississippi.

[45] Taliaferro County, Georgia.

[46] Madison County, Mississippi.

[47] A detailed statement of method and the analysis itself will be found in appendix H.

[48] Part of the cost of such practices is paid by the Agricultural Stabilization and Conservation Service in a program in which the Soil Conservation Service cooperates.

more, they reexamined their work with Negroes and noted that among those Negroes with whom SCS plans had been initiated a satisfactory number were applying conservation practices. This indicated, SCS officials said, that since service to a relatively small number of Negroes had been productive, additional effort to reach Negro owners with plans would bring in new active cooperators with the soil conservation programs.

The Commission found that the SCS for some time has made serious efforts to recruit more Negro professionals for its staff. Progress was being made toward desegregating work unit offices. A larger task remains to provide service on a nondiscriminatory basis which will not confine Negro professionals to working with Negroes or make the quantity and quality of service available to Negro landowners dependent upon the number of Negro staff members in a given area.

AGRICULTURAL STABILIZATION AND CONSERVATION SERVICE

The Agricultural Stabilization and Conservation Service (ASCS) is one of the most important agencies of the Department of Agriculture for those farmers in the South who are concentrated in the allotted crops—cotton, tobacco, and peanuts. This service, with offices in 3,000 counties, administers the crop allotment and price support programs and grants funds to farmers on a cost-share basis for the adoption of agricultural conservation practices.[49] The funds dispersed from these offices are so large that a distinguished commentator has noted "in many areas county government operations are dwarfed by ASC programs as measured in dollar expenditures or impact on residents or both." [50]

Those who administer this program in Washington and in State and area offices, including the areawide representatives called farmer fieldmen, are all employees of the Federal Government.

[49] *1965 Appropriations Hearings*, pt. 3, pp. 331–332, 341.

[50] Statement by Morton Grodzins in *Review of Farmers Committee System*, Report of the Study Committee (Washington, D.C., Nov. 28, 1962); pt. I, p. 46–I. Hereinafter referred to as *Report of the Study Committee*.

761–685 O—65——7

At the county level, however, a locally elected committee is interposed, which makes delicate decisions affecting the size of a farmer's allotment, on adjustments of program benefits between landlords and tenants, and on the appeals of farmers objecting to cuts in allotments. The county committee also hires the county staff whose salaries along with the cost of operating the county office are financed entirely by Federal funds.[51] The staff of the county ASC office has been in an anomalous position for some years. Although locally selected and not subject to the merit system or civil service, they have been given certain retirement and insurance benefits which Federal employees receive, and are covered by the nondiscriminatory employment requirements.[52] In each State there is a State ASC committee, appointed by the Secretary of Agriculture, responsible for supervising county committees and regulating elections of comunity and county committees. The State committee may determine whether community elections will be held by meeting, mail, or polling place.[53]

The Commission's study has indicated that the most serious problems of equal protection of the laws in the Agricultural Stabilization and Conservation Service programs are the exclusion of Negroes from the decision making of State and county committees and from employment in county offices. This is particularly notable since the main crops of the South for which allotments are established—cotton, tobacco, and peanuts—are much more important in the economic life of Negro farmers than of white farmers. It has been previously noted that 92 percent of Negro farmers are engaged in growing these crops and are, therefore, active participants in the programs administered by ASCS. Yet, of the 266,000 Negro farmers in the South not one had even been appointed to a State committee by the Secretary of Agriculture.[54]

---

[51] USDA, Commodity Stabilization Service, *County Administrative Handbook*, 1–CA (revision 1, as amended), pt. 4, par. 160.

[52] *Id.*, par. 220. *Report of the Study Committee, op. cit.*, pt. I, p. 8. Congressman Whitten, Chairman of the House Subcommittee on Agriculture Appropriations, noted that he considers the county staff to be ". . . full-time Federal employees whether so identified or not." *1964 Appropriations Hearings*, pt. 3, p. 1745.

[53] CSS *County Administrative Handbook, op. cit.*, pt. I, par. 12.

[54] *Letter from USDA to Commission*, Dec. 3, 1964.

In the past few years the Administrator of ASCS has appointed a number of Negroes to multicounty review panels from which committees are drawn to pass upon complaints arising from decisions of the county committees concerning acreage allotments, compliance, and other programs.

The County Committees

The real power in the ASCS program, however, is in the hands of county committees. These committees are usually elected indirectly by the vote of community committeemen who are directly elected in their communities. The ASC elections for community and county committeemen are entirely under the jurisdiction of the ASCS, are supervised by the State committee, and are conducted in accordance with detailed procedures.[55] In 1962 a committee appointed by the Secretary of Agriculture to review the farmer committee system recommended that elections should be entirely by mail ballot as "this type of election encourages more people to vote, and makes it more difficult for political and other organizations to dominate or influence the elections." [56] Responding to recommendations of the committee, the present administration has been encouraging increased participation in the elections. One of its most effective measures has been to require that tenants as well as landlords who have a share in the crop allotment receive notices of the elections and be eligible to participate.

One committee member, Professor Morton Grodzins, noted that not a single Negro had been elected to a county committee in the South. He stated that elections for such committees pose real difficulties because in a rural community powerful people "have a great opportunity to punish their local opponents with a wide range of economic, social, and political weapons." Professor Grodzins also maintained that "intimate acquaintanceship with and participation in the local community may lead not to even-handed justice but to subservience to the powerful and neglect of

---

[55] For the procedures governing community committeemen and county committee elections, see CSS *County Administrative Handbook*, *op. cit.*, pt. I.

[56] *Report of Study Committee*, *op. cit.*, p. 25.

the weak." [57] When a landlord-tenant relationship is added to the already powerful racial discrimination in Southern counties, the protection of the voting rights of Negro participants becomes of paramount importance if the ASCS committee system is to function properly.

Professor Grodzins' comments were given added emphasis in December 1964 when, out of 37,000 community committeemen and alternates elected to 7,400 community committees in the Deep South States, only about 75 were Negroes. Some of the reasons for the overwhelming disproportion in representation may be gathered from the circumstances surrounding the 1964 committee elections in Mississippi. There for the first time Negroes were elected to community committees in six counties. The election of this small group of Mississippi Negroes was the first break in what had previously been a solid wall of exclusion. Prior to this time the only Negro community committeemen elected in Mississippi came from one all-Negro community. The nomination of Negroes in this State came as the result of intensive activity by the Mississippi Summer Project of the Council of Federated Organizations (COFO) which succeeded in having Negroes nominated in nine counties. COFO representatives visited ASCS State and national officials and requested assurances that Negro voters would be protected and Negro nominees encouraged. Prior to the elections charges of intimidation of Negroes who had announced their candidacy were filed with ASCS and promptly investigated; steps were also taken by Department of Agriculture officials to reassure Negro nominees. On the day elections were held, COFO workers who attempted to act as poll-watchers and to observe the counting of ballots were arrested in a few instances and some were assaulted. At the time this Commission report was written, charges of intimidation and interference with Negro voters were still being investigated by ASCS. Prior to the election COFO had asked the Department of Agriculture to send observers from Washington to

[57] *Report of Study Committee,* Minority Report, p. 46–G.

the polling places. A representative of the State ASCS office was assigned to each county where Negroes were on the ballot and a Washington official was sent to the State office on election day.

In addition to the intimidation of some Negro nominees in Mississippi, the ASCS itself noted that some Negroes nominated in Alabama for community committeemen in the 1964 election had withdrawn their names.

Negro Personnel

When the Commission began its study of the ASCS, early in 1964, there were no Negroes employed in professional, clerical, or technical positions in the South, either in State or county positions. A few Negroes were employed on the custodial level. As of November 1964 the ASCS reported to the Commission that seven Negroes had been employed by county committees in temporary positions during the summer as compliance reporters, checking the acreage planted by farmers: two each in Arkansas, Louisiana, and Mississippi and one in Oklahoma. A GS–3 clerical worker had also been employed in the Kentucky State office. Thus, in over 1,350 offices in the Southern States, some of which had 10 or more employees, total permanent employment of Negroes by ASCS consisted of 1 full-time Grade 3 clerk and 7 part-time workers.

Service to Negroes

The Commission studied two basic programs of ASCS: the allocation of additional cotton allotments and the cost-sharing grants for agricultural conservation practices.

As a result of diversification to other enterprises, farmers in many counties do not raise all the cotton allotted to them and their acreage is released to the county committee in their own county or in other counties in the State which have requested it. The county committees which receive this released acreage then reapportion it among applicants who already have cotton allotments. At the request of the Commission the ASCS, which keeps no records of service by race, undertook to secure data from county offices. For eight counties a list of white and Negro applicants and recipients of released cotton allotments was prepared, with information on the amount requested and received, the size of original allotments, and the amount of total cropland.[58]

In three counties studied the percentage of Negro operators who applied for increased cotton acreage was smaller than that of whites. But in all counties the number of acres sought by Negro applicants was extremely small and in all counties the average Negro allotments, even after receipt of additional acreage, was less than 15 acres. The average total allotments of white farmers receiving additional cotton acreage was nowhere lower than 20 acres and ranged as high as 85 acres in a county where the Negro average was 9 acres. Thus, although Negroes received a proportionate share of their requests in these counties compared with whites, the actual amounts received did not contribute to a change in their economic position.[59]

On January 8, 1965, ASCS instituted a new policy regarding the reapportionment of cotton acreage.[60] Designed to enable a larger portion of released acreage to be made available to small farmers, it restricts the effective allotment for a farm to which released allotment is reapportioned to not more than 33 acres or 75 percent of the cropland for the farm, whichever is smaller.

---

[58] This analysis appears at app. I.

[59] The Commission did not determine whether applicants were advised in the county office as to the size of the requests they might make.

[60] USDA, ASCS, "Release and Reapportionment of Cotton Acreage Allotments," Notice CN-261, Jan. 8, 1965.

Average allotment of cotton acreage after reapportionment, by race of recipient, in selected counties, 1964

	White (acres)	Negro (acres)
Alabama:		
Hale	39.5	8.8
Sumter [1]	61.5	11.9
Georgia:		
Decatur	46.1	14.6
Lowndes	20.2	9.0
Mississippi:		
Holmes [1]	85.7	9.5
Leake	21.9	10.5
South Carolina:		
Berkeley	33.0	6.7
Williamsburg [1]	29.2	7.3

[1] Counties in which proportion of Negro operators applying for increased allotments was substantially lower than for whites.

In another program studied, the Commission found that in 1962 the ASCS encouraged its State directors to promote participation in the Agricultural Conservation Program (ACP) by farmers who had never before been participants. ACP is a cost-sharing grant program designed to assist farmers in adopting needed conservation practices. It is a cooperative effort with the Soil Conservation Service, which supervises the application of the practice. In 1962 the ASCS payments for ACP practices amounted to $212 million and was divided among 1.2 million participants. Of these, 200,000 were new participants.[61] The program was promoted by community committeemen. In Alabama certificates were awarded to committeemen who brought in five or more new participants. In some counties community committeemen were used to promote the ACP program for the first time. In one county the committeemen who secured the most new participants were awarded a trip to a convention at the Gulf Coast. In another county 10 percent of ACP funds were set aside for new participants.

In December 1962 the ASCS Washington office sought to determine to what extent Negroes had figured among the new par-

[61] *1965 Appropriations Hearings*, pt. 3, pp. 333, 395.

ticipants in the ACP program. Six States were asked to secure this information. All reported participation by Negroes in varying degrees. With the exception of Georgia, the States concerned reported that the numbers of Negroes among new participants appeared to be proportionate to their numbers among farm owners.[62] The manager of an Alabama ASCS county office estimated that in 1962 most of the new participants had been Negroes. A county extension agent in another county estimated that in 1962 over 75 percent of new participants in the ACP program were Negroes.

ASCS reported that in 1963 the number of new participants was only half that of the previous year.[63] Field interviews with ASCS officials indicated that the 1962 promotion was not repeated. Furthermore, the evaluation by the administrator of the participation by Negroes, which was the first of its kind, was cursory and did not act as a basis for further improvements in the administration of the program.

The active and positive response of county committees to the 1962 program to promote participation in the ACP program by farmers who had not previously availed themselves of its benefits is an excellent example of what can be done to reach small farmers by fixing a program objective, backed by the highest officials. But Commission field investigation indicated how important continued support of such an objective is if the program is not to be regarded as a "one-shot deal" as it was characterized by one official.

Summary

The virtual exclusion of Negroes from the ASCS structure poses one of the most serious problems with which the Department of Agriculture should be concerned, particularly since this exclusion is compounded by the discriminatory operation of the county committee elections. The lost opportunity to develop Negro leader-

---

[62] USDA, ASCS, Memorandum, Mar. 18, 1964 (copy retained in Commission files). The States reporting were Alabama, Georgia, Louisiana, Mississippi, North Carolina, and South Carolina.

[63] *1965 Appropriations Hearings*, p. 395.

ship, to further democratic procedures in Federal programs, and to accelerate the economic advancement of Negro farmers are the high costs of failure of ASCS to assume responsibility for the manner in which elections for its programs have been conducted in those areas of the country where Negroes have been denied the ballot.

Meanwhile, the persistence of an entirely white structure in county after county where the economic welfare of Negroes is being decided in their absence cannot help but raise questions as to the equity with which ASCS programs are being administered. Negroes have been further isolated by the fact that they have not been employed above the menial level in ASCS offices—one of the most important economic institutions in many rural towns.

The extension of economic benefits, through larger allotments and increased participation in cost-sharing grants, will require objective evaluation of the present situation and the establishment of increased participation by Negro farmers who are presently not part of the program as a continuing program goal.

IV. CONCLUSIONS, FINDINGS, AND RECOMMENDATIONS

CONCLUSIONS

For decades the general economic, social, and cultural position of the southern Negro farmer and rural resident in relation to his white neighbor has steadily worsened. Whether measured in terms of value of products sold, level of living, land and home ownership, or schooling, most of the 4.7 million Negroes living in southern rural areas are seriously disadvantaged when compared with rural white southerners.

Each census enumeration of population and agriculture has reflected the fact that the Negro farmers have not participated fully in the benefits of government programs and the progress of American agriculture. The continuing reliance of Negroes on cotton, tobacco, and peanuts in an economy where white farmers are rapidly diversifying to other farm enterprises has been shown in Government reports issued every 5 years. Statistics have attested to the shrinking acreage farmed by Negroes. Every 10 years the census has reported a widening gap in income, education, and housing between southern rural whites and Negroes.

Although small farmers, without regard to race, are rapidly decreasing in number and although economic pressures appear to be forcing a reduction in number and an increase in size of farms, there is unmistakable evidence that racial discrimination has served to accelerate the displacement and impoverishment of the Negro farmer.

For more than 100 years—and particularly during the past 30 years—the U.S. Department of Agriculture has administered federally financed programs designed to improve almost every aspect of the lives of low-income farm and rural families. Although other political, social, and economic factors have simultaneously operated to the disadvantage of the rural southern Negro, it should be a matter of national concern that the gap between Negro and white rural residents in the South has increased during the very period when the programs of the Department were helping thousands of rural white families to achieve substantial gains in income, housing, and education. As the group most depressed economically, most deprived educationally, and most oppressed socially, Negroes have been consistently denied access to many services, provided with inferior services when served, and segregated in federally financed agricultural programs whose very task was to raise their standard of living.

The Commission's analysis of four major U.S. Department of Agriculture programs has clearly indicated that the Department has generally failed to assume responsibility for assuring equal opportunity and equal treatment to all those entitled to benefit from its programs. Instead, the prevailing practice has been to follow local patterns of racial segregation and discrimination in providing assistance paid for by Federal funds. At the same time, the Department has not developed adequate procedures for evaluating the degree to which its programs reach Negro as well as white rural residents.

One result of this failure of responsibility has been the perpetuation of a double standard for southern Negroes and whites affected by the Department's programs. In the Cooperative Extension Service this has led to the creation of separate and unequal administrative structures providing inferior services to Negro farmers, youth, and homemakers. In the Farmers Home Administration, it has meant a different kind of service to the two races, with Negro farmers receiving for the most part subsistence loans with limited supervision, while white farmers received supervised loans for capital expenditures. In the Soil Conservation Service, the result has been little service at all to many Negro landowners in areas where no Negro staff members are employed.

As applied to staff, the double standard has taken various forms in the programs studied. These have included failure to recruit, employ, or upgrade Negroes, or to permit them to serve white farmers; isolation of Negroes in separate offices or at segregated meetings; and providing Negro staff members with inservice training of shorter duration and inferior content than that given white staff members. In State extension services Negro staff members have often been required to provide to Negro farmers technical services outside their area of training, while white farmers have received assistance from specialists in these areas.

In some programs, effective service to Negroes has been made dependent upon the number of Negroes employed, on the untenable theory that Negro farmers should be served only by Negro staff. This concept has worked to the detriment of both Negro rural families and Negro staff. Operating under this concept, these programs have failed to reach the Negro rural residents most in need of them because of inadequate numbers of Negro staff. At the same time, restricting Negro employees to serving only Negroes has further limited professional development and promotional opportunities.

Underlying much of the failure to provide equal service to Negro farmers in the South has been the preconception, found in the agricultural agencies, that Negro farmers have limited needs, capabilities, and aspirations. Starting with a view that Negroes cannot improve as farmers, many programs have not trained Negroes in the new technology nor encouraged them to diversify, to acquire larger acreage, or to make their small acreage more productive.

Relegated to a separate, inferior, and outdated agricultural economy, too many Negroes have sunk to lower levels of subsistence. When they failed as farmers and became landless, unskilled laborers, the Department has not helped them and their children make the transition to a new way of life.

One of the most serious obstacles barring Negro farmers from the benefits of the Department's programs has been the consistent exclusion of Negroes from the local decision-making process which controls the dispensing of these benefits. Negroes have not been appointed to State and local committees by the Department of Agriculture.

Prior to 1964, except in a few all-Negro towns, Negroes have not been candidates for locally elected committees. Almost without exception, Negroes do not join white farmers in making plans for the community. Originally built into the programs to assure flexibility and responsiveness to grassroots needs, these local controls have been used in the South to establish and maintain racial differentials in the kinds and amounts of Federal aid available to farmers. Far from discouraging such undemocratic practices in its programs, the Department itself has generally conformed to the discriminatory regional pattern.

The current unanimity of all branches of the Federal Government on the necessity for equal opportunity and equal treatment in the administration of Federal programs leaves no room for uncertainty concerning the aims of national policy as they relate to the Department of Agriculture. Some of the problems found in the Commission's study of the Department's programs will be reached by the requirement of Title VI of the Civil Rights Act of 1964 that federally assisted programs be administered without segregation or discrimination. Differential service, training, awards and activities, segregated offices, meetings, training, and competitions are outlawed by Title VI and the regulations of the Department of Agriculture issued thereunder. These regulations generally require immediate compliance, though the State extension services have been permitted a period of adjustment during which States must make necessary changes in offices, staffing and program.

In addition to the Civil Rights Act, the Federal Government has had a longstanding policy against the discrimination in employment which was found so prevalent in the agencies of the Department. Under Executive Order 10925, the policy prohibits segregated assignment of responsibilities and offices, limited promotion opportunities, and exclusion of Negroes from employment in other than menial capacities. Also, a White House directive against official participation by Federal employees in segregated meetings provides a clear mandate for conducting the educational and informational activities of the Department on a nondiscriminatory basis.

In enacting the Economic Opportunity Act of 1964, the Congress stated a further national objective: to eliminate "poverty in the midst of plenty in this Nation by opening to everyone the opportunity for education and training, the opportunity to work, and the opportunity to live in decency and dignity." The economically and socially deprived Negroes of the rural South stand in great need of such opportunities.

Federal laws and policies require the termination of segregation and discrimination in federally financed and administered agricultural programs. If the Department of Agriculture is to make its full contribution to the Nation's effort to revitalize rural America and to combat rural poverty, it must engage in a thorough-going critical evaluation of its programs. No rural renaissance is likely for the southern Negro so long as these programs continue to isolate him through entrenched discriminatory practices.

It is the Commission's belief that few of the economic problems now burdening the rural South can be solved until basic changes are made in the Federal programs designed to help bring about solutions. These changes must include the elimination of the segregated structuring of services, the removal of racial limitations on opportunity, and the inclusion in the decision-making process of broad sections of the population previously denied participation. Until these long-deferred changes are made, the South will continue to place a brake upon its own progress and that of the Nation.

FINDINGS

The Cooperative Extension Service

1. The federally assisted State extension services of the South are administered through a separate structure and generally on a discriminatory basis, often with separate and inferior offices for Negro staff.

2. With rare exceptions, at the county level, separate plans of work are usually made for services to Negroes in those counties where Negroes are employed as extension service personnel, and Negro and white staff do not plan extension programs or meet together.

3. Responsibility for work with Negro rural residents, in counties where Negro staff are employed, is assigned almost without exception to the Negro staff and the caseloads of Negro workers are so high as not to permit adequate service.

4. Negro Extension agents are denied access to training furnished their white coworkers and are confined largely to inferior training, except in North Carolina.

5. Many thousands of Negro youth are not served by extension services in counties where white youth are served, are denied access to national programs of the extension services through 4-H Clubs, and are denied the opportunity to compete with white youth for national and State awards of the 4-H program.

6. Many thousands of rural Negro homemakers receive less service than white homemakers in their counties, and in counties without Negro staff additional thousands are provided no service at all.

7. Many thousands of Negro farmers are denied access to services provided to white farmers which would help them to diversify, increase production, achieve adequate farming operations or train for off-farm employment.

761-685 O—65——8

8. No review or evaluation is conducted by the Federal Extension Service to ascertain the extent to which Negroes participate in extension service programs.

9. Services to Negroes tend to be limited by the preconception, expressed by many Federal, State, and county extension service officials, that Negroes as a class cannot succeed in agriculture or in productive ways of living.

10. Federal and State as well as local agriculture officials have participated and acquiesced in these discriminatory practices.

The Farmers Home Administration

1. The assistance rendered to Negroes by FHA in the form of loans and technical assistance is consistently different from that furnished to whites in the same economic class: Negro borrowers receive smaller loans, both absolutely and in relation to their net worth, than white farmers similarly situated. While carefully supervised white borrowers receive most of their funds for capital investments, including farm improvement or enlargement, Negroes in the same economic class, with drastically unequal supervision, receive loans primarily for living expenses and annual operating costs.

2. There is reason to believe that the type of loans made and the technical assistance given to Negroes is limited by preconceptions held by county personnel of the FHA that Negroes cannot successfully change the pattern of their farming operations.

3. A segregated service is maintained for those few Negroes employed by FHA in the South, confining them to work with Negroes, limiting their promotional opportunities, and housing them in offices separate from their white coworkers.

4. Negroes, with few exceptions, are not appointed as full members to county committees but are confined to a newly created category of special alternate membership.

The Soil Conservation Service

1. Negroes in southern counties generally receive less service from the SCS than whites, except in those counties where Negroes are employed as professionals.

2. Few Negroes are employed as soil conservationists in the South; among those who are so employed, some are housed in segregated offices and restricted in promotional opportunities.

3. Where Negro professionals are employed by the SCS in the South, they are generally confined to work with Negro landowners, and Negro landowners in these counties are restricted to receiving the services of Negro staff.

4. Negro professionals in the South do not participate in the deliberations of the boards of supervisors through which SCS services are channelled.

5. The SCS takes no responsibility for assuring participation by Negro landowners in conservation district elections for boards of supervisors; in southern counties where such boards are appointed, the SCS has not recommended Negroes for appointment. No Negro has been elected to a board of supervisors in the South.

6. No reviews or evaluations are conducted by the SCS to ascertain the extent to which Negroes participate in SCS programs.

The Agricultural Stabilization and Conservation Service

1. Until 1964, Negroes had not, with rare exceptions, participated in the nominations and elections under the supervision and jurisdiction of the Department for ASCS county committees in the South. ASCS did not assume responsibility for the elimination of discrimination in these elections prior to the winter of 1964. In that year, of 37,000 community committee members in the South, only 75 Negroes were elected. There were no Negroes among the almost 5000 county committeemen in 11 Southern States.

2. Negroes are not employed in permanent Federal or county ASCS positions in the South; nor are they appointed to important temporary positions filled each year by county committees.

3. No Negro has ever been appointed by the Secretary of Agriculture to a State ASC committee in the South.

4. No evaluation is conducted on a systematic basis to measure the impact of ASCS programs on white and Negro farmers or the extent to which farmers of both races participate in these programs.

RECOMMENDATIONS

The Commission Recommends

I. *That the President direct the Secretary of Agriculture to end discriminatory practices in the administration of Department programs,* and that the Secretary—

A. Continue efforts to impress upon the administrators and field staff of every agency the necessity of abandoning practices of segregation, unequal treatment, and exclusion which have barred Negro farmers and rural residents from the services and benefits of these programs.

B. Require the assignment to both white and Negro staff of the responsibility for work with Negro clientele participating in these programs.

C. Require the abolition of all racially segregated administrative structures and lines of authority, communication, and responsibility at Federal, State, and county levels.

D. Require that racial segregation of employees in Federal, State, and county offices be eliminated.

E. Require that all meetings connected with Department programs be held on a desegregated basis and that the Federal nondiscrimination policy be made known.

F. Enforce Department policy prohibiting employees from attending, participating in, or in any other way giving official support to organizations, meetings, fairs, or other events which are segregated, which exclude either Negroes or whites from membership, attendance or participation, or which are intended for participants of one race only.

II. *That the President direct the Secretary of Agriculture to encourage and extend full and equal participation in Department programs to all clientele without regard to their race or color,* and that the Secretary—

A. Direct every agency to seek increased participation by Negro farm and rural residents in those programs from which they previously have been excluded or in which they have been denied equitable service.

B. Afford to Negro farmers the necessary assistance, information, and encouragement to accord them the equal opportunity to diversify their farm enterprises.

C. Assure that Negroes have the opportunity to participate in elections for local committees and that they are appointed to State, area, and local committees which share responsibility for the administration of Department programs.

D. Provide adequate safeguards to assure that the administration of Department programs by local committees does not thwart the participation of Negroes.

III. *That the President direct the Secretary of Agriculture to assure equal employment opportunities in agricultural programs,* and that the Secretary—

Require that employment, training, assignment, and promotion of all personnel be based on merit and ability without regard to the race or color of the employee or of the clientele to be served.

IV. ***That the President direct the Secretary of Agriculture to establish methods for review and evaluation of implementation of equal opportunity policy in Department programs,*** and that the Secretary—

Use the research units of the Department to determine the extent to which agricultural programs are achieving their objectives with respect to individuals of all races and colors. For this purpose racial data and statistics on persons receiving the benefits of Department programs should be maintained as part of an effective reporting and evaluation system. Such data should be used only for the purpose of evaluating the effectiveness of Department programs and should be maintained under safeguards which will prevent their use for discriminatory purposes.

BIBLIOGRAPHY

PUBLIC DOCUMENTS

U.S. Bureau of the Census. *1959 Agriculture Census,* vols. I, II.

———. *1960 Census of Population.*

———. *1960 Census of Population. Subject Reports. Nonwhite Population by Race.*

———. *1960 Census of Housing,* vol. VI.

———. *Current Population Reports. Consumer Income: Income of Families and Persons in the United States: 1960.* Series P–60, No. 37, January 17, 1962.

———. *Current Population Reports. Farm Population: Estimates of the Farm Population of the United States: April 1963.* Series ERS P–27, No. 34, May 15, 1964.

———. Bressler, Tobia. "Some Population Trends Involving and Affecting the Negro—Implications," presented before the meeting of the *Association of Social Science Teachers.* Nashville, Tenn., March 22, 1962. (Mimeographed.)

U.S. Department of Agriculture. *Advance Report on the Hired Farm Working Force of 1962.* Economic Research Service, ERS–141, October 1963.

———. *Century of Service: the First 100 Years of the U.S. Department of Agriculture.* Washington: U.S. Government Printing Office, 1963.

———. *Directory of Organization and Field Activities of the Department of Agriculture.* Agricultural Handbook, No. 76, 1962.

———. *Economic Factors Influencing Attainments and Aspirations of Farm Youth.* Economic Research Service, Agricultural Economic Report, No. 51, April 1964.

——. *Farmers Home Administration in Brief* (PA 547). (Revised) February 1964.

——. *Loan Programs of the Farmers Home Administration,* June 1962.

——. *Recent Population Trends in the United States With Emphasis on Rural Areas,* Economic Research Service, Agricultural Economic Report No. 23, January 1963.

——. *What the Soil Conservation Service Does,* SCS–C1–3. (Revised) September 1963.

——. *You and the USDA,* 1963.

——. *A History of Agricultural Extension Work in the United States 1785–1923.* USDA Misc. Publ. No. 15. Prepared for the U.S. Department of Agriculture by Alfred Charles True. Washington: U.S. Government Printing Office, 192.

——. *Nature and Scope of Disadvantaged Rural Classes,* Economic Research Service, Farm Population Branch, March 7, 1963.

——. *The Cooperative Extension Service Today: A Statement of Scope and Responsibility,* April 1958.

——. *A Guide to Extension Programs for the Future: The Scope and Responsibilities of the Cooperative Extension Service,* July 1959.

——. *A Guide to Understanding the United States Department of Agriculture.* (Revised) October 1963.

——. *Rural Areas Development Handbook.* Agriculture Handbook No. 245, June 1963.

——. Commodity Stabilization Service. *County Administrative Handbook 1–CA* (Revision 1) as amended.

U.S. Congress, House of Representatives, Subcommittee of the Committee on Appropriations. *Hearings on the Department of Agriculture Appropriations for 1964.* (Parts 1–6) 88th Cong., 1st sess., 1963.

——. Subcommittee of the Committee on Appropriations. *Hearings on the Department of Agriculture Appropriations for 1965.* (Parts 1–6) 88th Cong., 2d sess., 1964.

———. Subcommittee of the Committee on Agriculture. *Hearings on Family Farms,* 88th Cong., 1st sess., 1963.

U.S. Department of Health, Education, and Welfare. Office of Education, *Statistics of Land-Grant Colleges and Universities.* Year ended June 30, 1962 (final report), OE–50002–62.

U.S. Department of Labor. *Manpower Report of the President and a Report on Manpower Requirements, Resources, Utilization, and Training,* March 1964.

U.S. Commission on Civil Rights. *Equal Protection of the Laws in Public Higher Education,* Washington: U.S. Government Printing Office, 1960.

BOOKS

Baker, Gladys. *The County Agent.* Studies in Public Administration, vol. XI. Chicago: University of Chicago Press, 1939.

Blair, Lewis H. *A Southern Prophecy: The Prosperity of the South Dependent Upon the Elevation of the Negro* (1889). Edited by C. Vann Woodward. Boston: Little, Brown & Co., 1964.

Eddy, Edward Danforth, Jr. *Colleges for Our Land and Time: The Land-Grant Idea in American Education.* New York: Harper & Bros., 1956.

Myrdal, Gunnar. *An American Dilemma.* New York: Harper & Bros., 1944.

Weaver, Robert C. *The Urban Complex: Human Values in Urban Life.* Garden City: Doubleday & Co., Inc., 1964.

REPORTS

Ornati, Dr. Oscar. *Poverty in America.* Report of the National Policy Committee on Pockets of Poverty, Farmers Educational Foundation. Washington: National Policy Committee on Pockets of Poverty, March 1964.

Review of the Farmer Committee System. Report of the Study Committee of the U.S. Department of Agriculture. Washington, November 28, 1962.

ARTICLES AND PERIODICALS

Cowhig, James D. and Beale, Calvin L. "Socioeconomic Differences Between White and Nonwhite Farm Populations in the South," *Social Forces,* 42, No. 3 (March 1964), pp. 354–362.

——. "Relative Socioeconomic Status of Southern Whites and Nonwhites, 1950 and 1960," *Southwestern Social Science Quarterly* (September 1964), pp. 113–124.

Davis, John W. "Land-Grant Colleges for Negroes." *West Virginia State College Bulletin,* Series 21, No. 5, April 1934.

"The American Farmer." Population Reference Bureau, Inc., *Population Bulletin,* XIX, No. 3 (May 1963), pp. 53–79.

The Farm Journal. March–September 1964.

OTHER SOURCES

County Agents Directory, 46th edition, Flossmoor, Ill.: C. L. Mast, Jr. and Associates, 1961.

County Agents Directory, 49th edition, Flossmoor, Ill.: C. L. Mast, Jr. and Associates, 1964.

APPENDICES

Appendix A. Sources of Funds Allotted for Cooperative Extension Work in 11 Southern States for the Fiscal Year Ending June 30, 1964

	Total funds	Total Federal funds	Total funds from within the States	
			State	County
Alabama	$5,109,906	$2,312,777	$1,879,126	$918,003
Arkansas	4,188,048	1,857,935	1,739,533	457,672
Florida	3,639,326	846,224	1,752,397	1,040,705
Georgia	6,013,082	2,424,745	2,285,025	1,249,562
Louisiana	4,760,186	1,524,892	2,921,751	298,900
Mississippi	4,713,255	2,382,855	1,438,400	870,600
North Carolina	8,569,847	3,235,825	3,095,687	2,201,376
South Carolina	3,108,190	1,693,920	1,244,000	169,070
Tennessee	4,730,410	2,353,310	1,708,615	668,485
Texas	8,381,208	3,739,043	2,132,740	2,480,375
Virginia	5,388,079	1,932,943	2,782,525	672,611
Total	$58,601,537	$24,304,469	$22,979,799	$11,027,359

PERCENT DISTRIBUTION

	Federal funds	Total funds from within the States	
		State	County
Alabama	45	37	18
Arkansas*	44	42	11
Florida	23	48	29
Georgia	40	38	21
Louisiana	32	61	6
Mississippi	50	31	19
North Carolina	38	36	26
South Carolina	55	40	5
Tennessee	50	36	14
Texas	45	25	30
Virginia	36	51	13

NOTES.—Figures rounded to nearest percent. Figures do not reflect value of office space when provided in county buildings, Federal buildings, and land-grant colleges.

*Arkansas reported 3.17 percent of funds from private sources; in other States this item was less than 1 percent.

Source: U.S. Congress, House, Subcommittee of Committee on Appropriations, *Hearings on Department of Agriculture Appropriations, 1965*, 88th Cong., 2d sess., pt. 2, p. 364.

Appendix B. Location of Offices of State Staff, Southern Extension Services

Alabama:

White staff: Alabama Polytechnic Institute, Auburn.

Negro staff: Tuskegee Institute, Tuskegee (private institution).

Florida:

White staff: University of Florida, Gainesville.

Negro staff: Florida A. & M. University, Tallahassee.

Georgia:

White staff: University of Georgia, Athens.

Negro staff: Fort Valley State College, Fort Valley.

Louisiana:

White staff: Louisiana State University.

Negro staff: Southern University (both at Baton Rouge).

Mississippi:

White staff: Mississippi State University, State College.

Negro staff: Jackson (not at a college).

North Carolina:

White staff: State A. & E. College, Raleigh.

Negro staff: A. & T. College, Greensboro.

South Carolina:

White staff: Clemson Agricultural College, Clemson.

Negro staff: State College, Orangeburg.

Tennessee:

White staff: University of Tennessee, Knoxville.

Negro staff: YMCA Building, Nashville.

Texas:

White staff: A. & M. College of Texas, College Station.

Negro staff: Prairie View A. & M., Prairie View.

Virginia:

White Staff: Virginia A. & M. College and Polytechnic Institute, Blacksburg.

Negro staff: Virginia State College, Petersburg.

Although Arkansas maintains a segregated system, its Negro State staff are at the white land-grant college in Fayetteville.

Source: *County Agents Directory,* 1964 (Chicago, C. L. Mast, Jr. Associates).

Appendix C

UNITED STATES DEPARTMENT OF AGRICULTURE
Office of the Secretary
Washington

June 23, 1964

MEMORANDUM TO: Assistant Secretaries
Agency Heads
Staff Assistants

SUBJECT: Federal Participation in Segregated Meetings

You are all certainly aware of the President's views that Federal officials should not participate in segregated meetings. It is the policy and goal of this Administration to secure equal treatment and equal opportunity for all Americans and to assure that no Federal program operates to encourage or support racial segregation. President Johnson has stated, "As far as the writ of Federal law will run, we must abolish not some but all racial discrimination."

Pursuant to this policy, government public information programs, educational activities and services of a like character should be available to all persons on an equal basis. Care must be exercised that acceptance of speaking engagements and participation in conferences by Federal officials is consistent with this policy. Officials should not participate in conferences or speak before audiences where any racial group has been segregated or excluded from the meeting, from any of the facilities or the conferences or from membership in the group.

When requests for speakers or participation are received under circumstances where segregation may be practiced, there is a clear obligation to make specific inquiry as to the practices of the group before acceptance is given. If the inviting group expresses a willingness to discuss modification of its practices for the occasion, obviously USDA should cooperate in such efforts.

The Federal government should not sponsor, support, or financially assist, directly or indirectly, any conference, convention or meeting held under circumstances where participants are segregated or are treated unequally because of race. This policy includes the granting of Federal funds to reimburse the expenditures of non-Federal agencies under grant-in-aid programs.

If the Federal civil rights program would be better served by permitting an exception to this policy in a particular case, the appropriate Assistant Secretary or Director should be advised prior to making any commitments for his confirmation of the waiver of the provisions of this directive.

Orville L. Freeman

Appendix D. Study of Extension Personnel Assignments in Selected Southern Counties by Race of Agent and Clientele

A study of extension service personnel assignment was made to determine whether there were significant differences in the assignment of white and Negro staff. The 25 counties in Alabama, Georgia, Louisiana, Mississippi, and South Carolina with the largest number of Negro farm operators were selected. Figure in parentheses indicates the smallest number of Negro farm operators in any county.

Alabama (*475*)	*Georgia* (*224*)	*Louisiana* (*280*)	*Mississippi* (*700*)	*South Carolina* (*490*)
Barbour	Baker [c]	Avoyelles [a]	Amite [a]	Aiken
Bullock	Bulloch [b]	Bienville [a]	Attala	Anderson
Butler	Burke [b]	Bossier [c]	Bolivar	Berkeley
Chambers	Decatur	Caddo	Chickasaw [c]	Chester
Choctaw	Early [c]	Claiborne [a]	Coahoma [a]	Chesterfield
Clarke [c]	Elbert [c]	Concordia [b]	DeSoto	Clarendon
Conecuh	Hancock	DeSoto [b]	Hinds	Colleton
Dallas	Hart [c]	East Carroll [b]	Holmes	Darlington
Elmore	Henry	East Feliciana [b]	Jefferson Davis	Dillon [c]
Greene	Jefferson [c]	Evangeline [c]	Kemper [c]	Dorchester
Hale	Lowndes	Franklin	Leake [a]	Edgefield [c]
Lee	Macon [c]	Lafayette [a]	Leflore	Florence
Limestone	Meriwether	Madison [a]	Lowndes [a]	Georgetown [a]
Lowndes	Mitchell [a]	Morehouse	Madison	Horry
Macon	Oglethorpe [c]	Natchitoches [a]	Marshall [a]	Kershaw
Madison	Randolph [c]	Pointe Coupee [b]	Monroe [a]	Laurens [b]
Marengo	Screven [b]	Richland [b]	Noxubee [a]	Lee [c]
Monroe	Stewart [c]	St. Helena [a]	Oktibbeha	Marion
Montgomery	Sumter	St. Landry	Panola	Marlboro [b]
Perry	Thomas	St. Martin [a]	Quitman	Orangeburg
Pickens [c]	Walton	Tangipahoa [a]	Sunflower	Richland
Pike [c]	Warren [c]	Tensas [b]	Tallahatchie	Spartanburg
Russell	Washington	Washington [b]	Tate [a]	Sumter
Sumter	Wilkes [c]	Webster [b]	Tunica [c]	Williamsburg
Wilcox	Worth [c]	West Feliciana [b]	Yazoo	York

[a] Indicates absence of Negro county agent.

[b] Indicates absence of Negro home demonstration agent.

[c] Indicates absence of both Negro county agent and Negro home demonstration agent.

The assignment of Negro and white extension personnel to these counties was then compared to the number of farm operators, rural households, and rural youth of 4-H Club age (10-19 years)[1] by race to ascertain the ratios of extension personnel to clientele. Male county agents were compared to farm operators and male youth, and female extension staff were compared to rural households and female youth.

Ratios were computed of extension workers to clientele by race in counties with both white and Negro extension personnel.

Ratios were computed of white extension workers to white clientele, and of white extension workers to white and Negro clientele combined in counties with no extension personnel assigned to work with Negroes.

Table I shows numbers of farm operators, rural youth, rural households, and extension personnel by race in those counties studied with both white and Negro extension staff.

Table II shows numbers of farm operators, rural youth, rural households, and extension personnel by race in those counties studied without Negro extension staff.

Table III shows number of farm operators, rural youth and rural households for each extension worker by race in selected counties without Negro staff, with potential caseloads for white workers if white and Negro clientele are combined.

---

[1] *County Agents Directory, 1964, supra; 1959 Agriculture Census,* vol. I, county table 3; and *Census of Population, 1960,* PC(1)–B, table 29. There have been reductions in number of white and Negro extension staff, in number of farm operators, and in number of rural households since the time of enumeration.

Table I.—*Number of farm operators, rural households, rural youth, and extension staff in selected counties of 5 Southern States by race for counties with both white and Negro extension workers*

State	Number of studied counties with both white and Negro county agents	Number of farm operators		Number of rural male youth 10–19 years		Number of county agents	
		White	Negro	White	Negro	White	Negro
Alabama	22	18,085	20,684	18,734	31,265	58	26
Georgia	12	8,602	4,471	8,860	10,459	22	12
Louisiana	14	13,744	8,879	15,016	16,920	40	14
Mississippi	14	13,004	20,041	13,233	28,480	42	21
South Carolina	21	28,438	21,726	54,997	45,242	58	23

State	Number of studied counties with both white and Negro home demonstration agents	Number of rural households		Number of rural female youth 10–19 years		Number of home demonstration agents	
		White	Negro	White	Negro	White	Negro
Alabama	22	57,391	50,320	17,097	29,601	40	22
Georgia	10	20,956	13,105	6,754	7,887	13	10
Louisiana	13	54,388	27,292	17,839	15,626	28	13
Mississippi	22	52,053	65,086	16,951	37,605	43	25
South Carolina	20	118,772	62,681	43,032	42,373	37	21

Sources: *1959 Agriculture Census*, vol. I, county table 3. *Census of Population, 1960*, PC(1)-B, table 29. *County Agents Directory, 1964*.

Table II.—*Number of farm operators, rural households, rural youth, and extension staff in selected counties of 5 Southern States by race for counties without extension personnel assigned to work with Negroes*

State	Number of studied counties without Negro county agents	Number of farm operators		Number of rural male youth 10–19 years		Number of county agents	
		White	Negro	White	Negro	White	Negro
Alabama	3	2, 854	1, 885	2, 697	2, 757	8	....
Georgia	13	7, 113	3, 812	5, 776	8, 045	14	....
Louisiana	11	14, 060	5, 334	13, 983	9, 103	30	....
Mississippi	11	10, 036	12, 803	7, 680	14, 478	25	....
South Carolina	4	2, 918	3, 151	3, 434	6, 007	9	....

State	Number of studied counties without Negro home demonstration agents	Number of rural households		Number of rural female youth 10–19 years		Number of home demonstration agents	
		White	Negro	White	Negro	White	Negro
Alabama	3	7, 454	4, 947	2, 467	2, 747	6	....
Georgia	15	18, 948	15, 838	6, 971	21, 056	17	....
Louisiana	12	27, 537	20, 418	9, 370	11, 156	22	....
Mississippi	3	4, 393	5, 256	1, 387	2, 974	4	....
South Carolina	5	14, 374	9, 703	5, 709	6, 692	8	....

Sources: *1959 Agriculture Census*, vol. I, county table 3. *Census of Population, 1960*, PC(1)–B, table 29. *County Agents Directory, 1964*.

Table III.—*Number of farm operators and rural boys aged 10–19 years, for each male extension worker, by race, in selected counties without Negro staff*

State	Farm operators		Rural boys	
	White	White and Negro	White	White and Negro
Alabama	357	592	337	682
Georgia	508	840	413	1, 126
Louisiana	469	646	466	770
Mississippi	401	914	307	860
South Carolina [a]	324	674	382	1, 049

Number of rural households and rural girls aged 10–19 years, for each female extension worker, by race, in selected counties without Negro staff

State	Rural households		Rural girls	
	White	White and Negro	White	White and Negro
Alabama	1, 242	2, 066	411	869
Georgia	1, 115	2, 046	410	1, 649
Louisiana	1, 252	2, 180	426	933
Mississippi	1, 098	2, 412	273	860
South Carolina [a]	1, 797	3, 010	714	1, 550

[a] Although the caseload of white workers in South Carolina would be very heavy if Negroes were included, it does not exceed that of white workers in counties with Negro staff. However, as table 1 in the text shows, caseloads of white workers in South Carolina are extremely high compared to those in the other studied States.

Appendix E. Federal and Non-Federal Contributions of Funds to Soil and Water Conservation Districts Program, Fiscal Year 1963

State	Federal	State and local government	Percentage of Federal funds
Alabama	$2, 509, 038	$206, 800	92
Arkansas	5, 566, 374	1, 300, 900	81
Florida	2, 189, 814	418, 900	84
Georgia	5, 970, 256	1, 160, 800	84
Kentucky	4, 252, 793	588, 400	88
Louisiana	2, 929, 484	1, 711, 500	63
Mississippi	7, 286, 078	303, 700	96
North Carolina	3, 368, 671	1, 253, 600	73
South Carolina	2, 786, 543	242, 900	92
Texas	23, 530, 788	1, 205, 000	95
Virginia	2, 721, 498	259, 700	91
Total	$63, 111, 337	$8, 652, 200	88

Source: USDA, SCS, "Detailed Statement of Obligations by Geographic Location" and Advisory DIST–2, Jan. 24, 1964, memorandum to State conservationists, "Districts—Estimate of Non-Federal Contributions to Soil and Water Conservation Districts, Fiscal Year 1963."

Appendix F. Number of Part- and Full-Owner Operators and Number of Soil Conservation Service Plans, by Color of Operator

State and county	Number of operators	Number of SCS plans	Number of operators	Number of SCS plans	Number of SCS plans per 100 operators	
	White		Negro		White	Negro
Alabama:						
Dallas	503	564	602	100	112	16
Greene	265	410	358	105	151	29
Hale	540	489	596	110	90	18
Macon	381	388	644	100	102	15
Perry	412	648	465	109	158	23
Sumter	367	449	389	190	121	48
Wilcox	419	547	492	178	133	36
Arkansas:						
Crittendon [1]	265	202	266	183	75	68
Jefferson	456	515	366	80	112	22
Lee [1]	416	944	494	220	230	44
Phillips [1]	395	454	545	160	114	30
Florida:						
Alachua	797	681	213	30	85	14
Jackson	1,370	800	548	100	58	19
Marion	1,249	391	356	13	32	4
Georgia:						
Burke	347	594	246	137	175	57
Decatur	634	473	187	22	75	11
Lowndes	591	489	194	46	82	23
Taliaferro	110	408	79	98	370	124
Kentucky:						
Christian	1,394	828	162	29	59	15
Louisiana:						
Bossier	584	573	489	101	96	20
De Soto	810	824	547	152	10	28
St. Landry	1,897	739	642	69	39	11
Maryland:						
Calvert	526	383	200	24	74	12
Charles	676	414	139	18	59	14
Prince Georges	721	327	171	11	45	6

See footnotes at end of table.

State and county	Number of operators	Number of SCS plans	Number of operators	Number of SCS plans	Number of SCS plans per 100 operators	
	White		Negro		White	Negro
Mississippi:						
Clay	522	411	393	68	79	17
Holmes	596	442	742	252	74	34
Jasper	1, 151	434	520	61	36	12
Jefferson Davis	852	695	713	186	77	26
Kemper	754	298	423	93	37	22
Leake	1, 532	364	594	30	24	5
Madison	596	493	782	356	82	45
Marshall	503	445	458	250	89	50
Oktibbeha	637	497	496	60	79	12
Pike	945	630	611	69	67	11
Walthall	1, 156	649	499	60	54	12
Winston	1, 232	274	479	28	22	6
North Carolina:						
Bertie	639	458	515	80	73	16
Brunswick	990	279	456	25	28	5
Columbus [1, 2]	2, 785	595	815	68	21	8
Duplin	2, 236	513	793	12	23	2
Halifax [2]	665	650	734	127	93	17
Hertford	276	719	261	90	240	30
Warren [2]	435	592	683	215	138	31
South Carolina:						
Beaufort	126	145	415	28	121	7
Berkley	643	475	1, 090	88	74	8
Clarendon	678	510	628	96	73	15
Fairfield	348	596	309	72	175	24
Georgetown	434	284	462	61	66	12
Jasper	185	194	289	27	97	9
Orangeburg	1, 467	731	949	31	49	3
Sumter	566	446	778	164	74	21
Williamsburg	1, 066	688	1, 183	40	63	3
Tennessee:						
Fayette	649	239	441	23	40	5
Haywood	680	771	370	102	110	26
Madison [1]	1, 113	1, 251	375	298	113	7
Shelby	1, 128	671	534	20	60	5

See footnotes at end of table.

State and county	Number of operators	Number of SCS plans	Number of operators	Number of SCS plans	Number of SCS plans per 100 operators	
	White		Negro		White	Negro
Texas:						
Marion	192	371	163	64	186	32
Virginia:						
Brunswick	705	557	532	160	80	30
Cumberland	346	245	308	40	72	13
Dinwiddie[1]	592	716	390	185	119	46
Greensville	286	257	236	45	86	20
King and Queen	345	126	225	14	37	6
Lunenburg	644	454	301	80	71	25
Mecklenburg	1, 048	747	561	60	72	10
Surry	229	268	180	49	122	25
Sussex	292	289	233	41	96	18
Total	47, 148	34, 003	31, 041	6, 303	72	20

[1] Negro soil conservationist assigned.

[2] Includes Indians (not more than 10 percent).

NOTE.—Where more SCS plans are reported than the total number of owners and part owners, this is explained by the fact that plans are made for operating units, and a farmer may have 2 or more parcels of land. Also, SCS makes plans for nonfarmland and land not reported as farmland in the census. Since there is no report of ownership of nonfarmland by race, comparisons had to be limited to farmland.

Sources: Number of operators: *Census of Agriculture, 1959*, vol. I, county table 3. Number of plans: U.S. Department of Agriculture, Soil Conservation Service, *Work Unit Estimates of Assistance to Negro Cooperators*.

Appendix G. Number of Acres in Farms, Number of Acres Planned by Soil Conservation Service, and Percent of Acres in Plans by Color of Owner-Operators

State and county	Acres in farms		Acres in SCS plans		Percent of acres planned	
	White	Negro	White	Negro	White	Negro
Alabama:						
Dallas	334,017	44,088	284,160	8,000	85	18
Greene	187,098	39,864	171,175	16,800	92	42
Hale	203,791	35,454	141,598	9,350	70	26
Macon	172,071	48,076	134,088	12,800	78	27
Perry	212,685	38,830	198,571	11,118	93	29
Sumter	241,152	39,661	167,554	15,200	70	38
Wilcox	301,727	34,930	168,803	13,172	56	38
Arkansas:						
Crittenden [1]	195,575	17,620	161,046	13,359	82	76
Jefferson	159,231	20,836	190,900	6,640	120	32
Lee [1]	147,459	34,319	224,292	17,820	152	52
Phillips [1]	147,653	47,391	183,438	11,200	124	24
Florida:						
Alachua	307,380	15,257	198,291	1,500	65	10
Jackson	270,077	43,005	189,600	12,000	70	28
Marion	399,326	19,102	142,302	1,118	36	6
Georgia:						
Burke	231,545	33,945	258,462	17,125	112	50
Decatur	194,882	14,931	214,368	3,432	110	23
Lowndes	144,004	16,816	173,785	4,370	121	26
Taliaferro	33,303	7,952	70,244	12,740	211	160
Kentucky:						
Christian	254,079	12,545	176,068	3,045	69	24
Louisiana:						
Bossier	187,769	18,728	169,044	4,848	90	26
De Soto	231,745	32,403	175,840	11,552	76	36
St. Landry	173,802	23,098	113,178	3,174	65	14

See footnotes at end of table.

State and county	Acres in farms		Acres in SCS plans		Percent of acres planned	
	White	Negro	White	Negro	White	Negro
Maryland:						
Calvert	65, 055	8, 160	43, 785	1, 392	67	17
Charles	101, 906	7, 652	84, 078	1, 026	83	13
Prince Georges	72, 104	7, 501	56, 594	528	79	7
Mississippi:						
Clay	130, 857	30, 570	102, 001	6, 732	78	22
Holmes	273, 124	67, 044	118, 392	23, 184	43	35
Jasper	191, 741	37, 775	65, 593	4, 697	34	12
Jefferson Davis	128, 254	52, 217	89, 450	14, 508	70	28
Kemper	156, 909	49, 342	62, 701	10, 416	40	21
Leake	161, 167	42, 565	36, 114	1, 710	22	4
Madison	206, 380	63, 748	111, 333	49, 128	54	77
Marshall	187, 608	53, 845	90, 035	23, 250	48	43
Oktibbeha	135, 696	36, 104	95, 460	4, 800	70	13
Pike	127, 068	35, 094	86, 352	7, 314	68	21
Walthall	153, 387	30, 170	83, 498	3, 000	54	10
Winston	163, 832	33, 051	36, 858	2, 100	23	6
North Carolina:						
Bertie	108, 906	34, 832	98, 496	4, 800	90	14
Brunswick	91, 484	18, 228	27, 576	1, 000	30	6
Columbus [1, 2]	223, 889	29, 564	62, 067	2, 244	28	8
Duplin	242, 117	29, 079	75, 645	480	31	2
Halifax [2]	170, 978	48, 515	129, 461	11, 176	76	23
Hertford	44, 924	20, 973	106, 780	6, 480	238	31
Warren [2]	88, 401	43, 760	74, 792	10, 750	85	25
South Carolina:						
Beaufort	53, 341	8, 521	123, 053	1, 680	231	20
Berkeley	84, 690	25, 842	153, 240	4, 400	181	17
Clarendon	145, 424	36, 479	129, 654	9, 120	89	25
Fairfield	133, 372	29, 514	127, 632	8, 640	96	29
Georgetown	56, 058	13, 438	41, 924	1, 891	75	14
Jasper	46, 736	10, 605	203, 235	2, 295	435	22
Orangeburg	359, 455	51, 952	160, 061	3, 007	45	6
Sumter	141, 901	43, 901	103, 180	13, 940	73	32
Williamsburg	248, 029	55, 264	123, 512	3, 160	50	6
Tennessee:						
Fayette	183, 215	39, 337	50, 394	2, 530	28	6
Haywood	150, 424	24, 945	148, 755	12, 750	99	51
Madison [1]	178, 455	27, 764	176, 636	24, 734	99	89
Shelby	180, 559	22, 689	89, 021	1, 500	49	7

See footnotes at end of table.

State and county	Acres in farms		Acres in SCS plans		Percent of acres planned	
	White	Negro	White	Negro	White	Negro
Texas:						
Marion	39,360	12,736	106,368	4,992	270	39
Virginia:						
Brunswick	138,147	32,460	91,965	12,000	67	37
Cumberland	86,775	17,154	43,655	2,800	50	16
Dinwiddie [1]	114,616	27,088	95,026	18,500	83	68
Greensville	62,734	20,894	38,236	4,950	61	24
King and Queen	62,077	13,673	36,638	1,442	59	11
Lunenburg	110,635	23,597	66,760	8,000	60	34
Mecklenburg	169,928	38,094	108,987	4,800	64	13
Surry	47,828	14,623	56,353	5,145	118	35
Sussex	91,239	20,146	69,697	4,223	76	21

[1] Negro soil conservationist assigned.

[2] Includes Indians (not more than 10 percent.)

NOTE.—Where more than 100 percent of white-owned farmland is reported as under SCS plan, this arises from the fact that SCS makes plans for land not reported as farmland by the census and for nonagricultural land. However, since there is no report of ownership of nonfarmland by race, comparisons were limited to farmland.

Sources: *1959 Agriculture Census*, vol. I county table 3. Figures for full- and part-owners were used. U.S. Department of Agriculture, Soil Conservation Service, Resource Development Division, *Work Unit Estimates of Assistance to Negro Cooperators and Application of Indicator Practices by Negro Cooperators*, June 1964.

Appendix H. Percent of Negro Farms and Acreage in Selected Size Ranges of Farms and Percent of Application of Conservation Practices in Such Farms for 6 Counties in Alabama

County	Size of farm (acres)		Conservation practice	Percent of farms owned [1]	Percent of acreage owned	Percent of conservation practice applied [2]
	Census	SCS				
Dallas	50–139	50–150	Pasture and hayland planting	62.4	62	33
Greene	100–219	100–200	Farm ponds	48.5	....	17
Hale	50– 99	60–100	Terraces	61.6	68	49
Perry	60–100	80	Pasture and hayland planting	64.1	68	33
Sumter	70–139	80–120	Farm ponds	59.5	....	18
Wilcox	50– 99	50–100	Pasture and hayland planting	67.2	69	43

[1] Distribution of white and Negro farms by acreage was derived by applying proportions prevailing in the economic area of which these counties are a part. The counties listed are 6 of the 10 counties in the State economic area.

[2] This estimate was made by the Soil Conservation work units.

Source: *1959 Agriculture Census*, unpublished data for Alabama State Economic Area No. 5 and Soil Conservation Service, *Work Unit Estimates of Service to Negroes*, 1964.

Appendix I. Acreage in Cropland, Original Cotton Allotment, and Acreage Received on Reapportionment of Allotments, by Race of Recipient, 1964, for Selected Counties

[Acres]

State and county	Average received on reapportionment		Average original allotment		Total allotment after reapportionment		Average acreage in cropland	
	White	Negro	White	Negro	White	Negro	White	Negro
Alabama:								
Hale	7.3	2.2	32.2	6.6	39.5	8.8	125.2	24.2
Sumter	13.7	3.5	47.7	8.4	61.4	11.9	255.9	36.5
Georgia:								
Decatur	26.0	5.9	20.1	8.7	46.1	14.6	230.3	81.3
Lowndes	10.8	4.6	9.4	4.4	20.2	9.0	120.8	41.7
Mississippi:								
Holmes	4.5	.7	81.2	8.8	85.7	9.5	301.6	40.2
Leake	7.3	3.2	14.6	7.3	21.9	10.5	58.9	26.0
South Carolina:								
Berkeley	12.6	2.4	20.4	4.3	33.0	6.7	107.8	17.1
Williamsburg	5.8	1.2	23.4	6.1	29.2	7.3	113.9	25.6

Source: USDA, ASCS, *Information Relating to Release and Reapportionment of 1964 Cotton Acreage.*

U.S. GOVERNMENT PRINTING OFFICE: 1965 O—761-685